upS____ng

80 MINDFUL PRACTICES TO SHIFT YOUR LIFE FROM BLUES TO BLISS

May all the bliss in the world be yours!

Tamra

TAMRA FLEMING

The material in this book is intended to offer an overview of spiritual and metaphysical philosophies. There are various opinions regarding this material and the author's intent is to only offer information of a general nature to help you in your journey for emotional and spiritual well-being. The content of this book is written for educational purposes only. The author does not dispense advice or prescribe the use of any technique as a form of treatment for physical, mental, or emotional problems, and suggests the reader seek professional advice of a physician or mental health professional to address these issues. If any of the information in this book is used for yourself, which is your constitutional right, the author and publisher assume no responsibility for your actions.

For Terry,
the one person in this world who kept the light shining for me in my darkest hours and lifted me gently from the blues with his undying love and sense of humor.
My bliss is you.

For Veronica,
my one sister who took me into her heart and gave unceasingly of her time, energy, home, and soul. Her faith held me up when I had lost mine.
My eternal gratitude is for you.

Table of Contents

Gratitude

A book is never written alone. There are many people across time who impact the content, shape, and message of any book, especially one on personal growth. This book is no different. The people I mention below all held my heart in a sacred way while I navigated the darkest period of my life. Without them, I would be someone else, somewhere else—quite possibly without the glow that their love and support offered to me in my sacred time of transformation.

When you face a crisis, you know
who your true friends are.

—Magic Johnson

Thank you, my dear friends, for loving and supporting me without judgment and with the deepest compassion. While the journey is a solo adventure, it takes a village, as we are all one. We are never alone, you made sure of that.

Deborah Garraway Buchta, who loved me back to earth.

Teryl Jackson, who held the light as a kindred sister for a positive day.

Pattie Hanmer, who called me frequently, so that I never felt alone.

Sandi Hanson, who is my soul sister, witness, and sacred holder of the light within the dark.

Rod Hanson, who was my sacred, safe witness to the journey.

Gabriella Delphia, who lovingly helped me through the chaos of the dark.

Sharon Crawford, who held my heart in her sacred, sweet, nurturing way.

Melody Biringer, who walked with me in the truth of my reality.

Lee Ladyga, who always held an outstretched heart and open ears to listen.

Jim Taylor, who propped me up when I no longer felt I could.

Brenda Reiss, who is a kindred soul sister of light and comrade on the path.

Robin Perdomo, who held my heart and shuttled me to and fro.

Rebecca Lellek, who was a compassionate witness and keeper of the light.

Kendra E Thornbury, who fiercely held my spirit in the highest potential for transformation.

Jennifer Kilpatrick, who lovingly sat at my bedside and deeply listened.

Mitzi Garnett, who, no matter what, is always there as a warrior sister for life.

Roger Nyhus, who is the brother I never had.

Steve Weber, who traveled alongside me comparing notes and creating a new life.

Teresa Bryant, who walked with me as we each made sense of the journey.

Matt Bryant, who was there when I felt confused and lost.

Karen McNenny, who listened deeply and held great compassion.

Dave Schultz, who held a higher knowing with a graceful heart and open ears.

I Serenity, who dove with me into the depth of the story while holding the light.

Amanda Larrinaga, who was there to encourage and witness my rising from the ashes.

14

Dr. Janel Jones, who cared for the recovery of my body, mind, and soul.

Cyndi Padilla, who reminded me of the love of God and was a sacred witness to my return to faith.

Sally Kirk, who is a forever friend and always holds a state of grace and love.

Rachel Kirk, who is a courageous sister traveler waging her own war with the body, mind, and soul.

Sue Richards, who has held open the gate to the personal path of sacred transformation.

Thank you to my family who picked me up and propped me up so that I could face the truth and heal. There are no words that can describe my deep gratitude for your part in my life's journey.

My one true sister of the heart, *Veronica Fleming*
My beautiful and brilliant niece, *Mckenzie Stott*
My fearless nephew, *Mark Stott*
My fierce warrior dad, *Mark Fleming*
My encouraging and loving mother, *Juanita Fleming*

And my deep gratitude goes to my writing team who traveled with me on the fierce journey of writing my first book—*Veronica Fleming, Fawn McManigal, Rachel Vdolek, Lauren Head,* and *Lori Ference,* for without them this book would never have seen the light of day.

I am truly blessed.

Introduction

The master sees beyond what is obvious. He sees the unseen, feels the unfelt, and hears the unheard. He looks below the surface for what is hidden and so finds the great heartbeat of the Universe. He smiles, knowing it is his heartbeat, your heartbeat, our heartbeat.

—Wu Wei

An Invitation to Bliss

This book is designed to lift your spirits and provide you with tools, tips, and affirmations to consistently be the extraordinary human that you are in your heart. Whether you're just needing a boost of inspiration or truly feeling blue, I invite you to explore these pages and find what speaks to you. The journey to bliss can be as short as one choice made in the now. It's accessible to you whenever you choose. This is your co-creative universe!

Great Change Is Afoot

Are you feeling it? If you've had the experience of being challenged, tested, frustrated, in a state of confusion, or in a bit of misery lately, you're not alone. We are in a stage of human evolution that is pushing to the surface what no longer serves humanity or Mother Earth.

Every negative emotion, from a lack of integrity, judgment, control, resentment, blame, and victimhood, is up for review. Human struggle, egoic actions, repeated patterns, well-worn stories, addiction to drama, and misused personal energy are all outdated mindsets of humanity. We are in uncharted territory and have been tapped to awaken.

80 Unique Gifts Inside

If you have been experiencing the *blues*—disappointment, frustration, mild depression, isolation, separation—it may be your wake-up call to take responsibility for your life force and move toward a more harmonious life. I say it "may be" because there is never a straight line through personal transformation. Life is riddled with a vast range of experiences from grief to glee. These experiences inform your life story—where you are presently, what you're thinking, and what you're choosing at the time. You are not broken; you may just need a lift.

This book is *not* about positive thinking or trying to be happy all of the time; it's about embracing life, taking 100% responsibility for your choices, and striving for a new way of being—more conscious, illuminated.

These pages offer 80 mindful practices for you to consider as you navigate every precious day of your own personal evolution. If you need simple practices, useful affirmations, and tools to reset your thinking, then you're in the right place.

How This Book Came to Be

It has been a struggle for me to maintain a consistent spiritual practice. I've often lacked commitment and discipline. I've been a seeker—from bible studies to sweat lodges, evangelistic gatherings to soulful sing-alongs, born again surrendering to heart-cracking moments with Jesus, shamanic vision quests and fire walking to Tibetan faith healing, bliss-filled realizations to the deepest dark night of the soul. I learned that *seeking is searching* and *being is being*. Even with all the seeking, I still couldn't figure out how to come home to my most divine self.

I once had a Buddhist Nun look me in the eyes and ask, "Do you want the knowledge, or do you want to live it, to be it?" That question catapulted my spiritual quest in a new direction, and with one goal: to *be* it, to *be* the best human reflection of God's love I could possibly be.

It became obvious to me that I was to embark on a journey filled with unknown challenges and trials. I expected to experience ups and down, tests and tribulations, lessons and losses, committed experiments and failed attempts. But I did not anticipate the arrival of a sweeping, limitless human experience that spans from pure joy to the doorstep of death.

The only way I could have written this book is because I've visited *the dark place*, and I have experienced *wordless bliss*—both ends of the spectrum of life—but not in the order you might think.

Bliss First

Sean Meshorer, the author of *The Bliss Experiment: 28 Days to Personal Transformation*, describes bliss like this: "It is a state of unity, transcendence, completeness, knowingness, wholeness, and uplifted consciousness; it is a feeling of oneness and connection with all of creation."

18

I experienced this state of bliss for a handful of days during the peak of my intense spiritual practice. My heart felt as vast as the universe. I had no words to describe what I was feeling and joyful tears flowed down my face most of the time. I sat nose-to-nose with my teacher and just nodded, *yes, yes, yes*. I kept saying, "Everyone needs to know this." Bliss and an open heart filled with love, compassion, and indescribable oneness was all I felt.

To my mind, I had truly experienced bliss, and couldn't imagine other people in the world not feeling this way too. What a place to be! Then my teacher gave me a choice: "You can either stay in this state, or you can come out and go back to work on yourself." As a spiritual warrior seeking enlightenment, I of course came out of this state to continue working on cracking the code of my subconscious habits and creative ego.

Into the Dark

Madisyn Taylor of *DailyOM* describes the dark night of the soul well. She says,

> A dark night of the soul is a very specific experience that some people encounter on their spiritual journeys. There are people who never encounter a dark night of the soul, but others must endure this as part of the process of breaking through to the dawn of higher consciousness. The dark night of the soul invites us to fully recognize the confines of our ego's identity. We may feel as if we are trapped in a prison that affords us no access to light or the outside. We are coming from a place of higher knowing, and we may have spent a lot of time and energy reaching toward the light of higher consciousness. This, is why the dark night has such a quality of despair. We are suddenly shut off from what we thought we had realized and the emotional pain is very real. We may even begin to feel that it was all an illusion and that we are lost forever in this darkness. The more we struggle, the darker things get, until finally we surrender to our not

19

knowing what to do, how to think, where to turn. It is from this place of losing our sense of ourselves as in control that the ego begins to crack or soften and the possibility of light entering becomes real. Some of us will have to endure this process only once in our lives, while others may have to go through it many times. The great revelation of the dark night is the releasing of our old, false identity. We finally give up believing in this false self and thus become capable of owning and embracing the light.

It wasn't until I had a deep, *dark night of the soul* experience that I was able to understand the dimensions one could travel. I thought I'd had dark nights before, but this was the real deal; it was different. It lasted three years from start to finish. It was the most tumultuous, distressing time of my life. It was self-inflicted and by divine design.

At first, my mind started to break down. I had made some life choices that were questionable, all in the name of spiritual evolution. These choices were so unorthodox that I had become extremely isolated. Cut off from my spiritual rudder, I panicked and grasped for purpose and meaning in my life.

Then my body broke down. I injured my knee, lost the vision in my left eye, acquired a mysterious autoimmune disorder, thought I'd had a series of heart attacks, and experienced a myriad of other physical issues. As I struggled with doctors, MRIs, cardiac tests, a spinal tap, medications, and ineffective treatments, I kept thinking about how I had the knowledge to heal myself and wondered why I couldn't, or why I chose not to. I could have pulled myself out of the chaos but I didn't.

Why? Because my false self—my ego—was still desperately seeking someone or something outside of myself to save me. I had put the responsibility for healing and self-care on others. I was not embracing the idea that as a co-creator with God I could heal. That required faith. Where was my faith?

I had learned that my spiritual teacher, to whom I entrusted my spiritual growth, had hidden a truth. His deceit crushed my trust. How could I not see this charade? How could I have gone outside of my own inner guidance system and trust his more than mine? How could I give my power away to anyone but God? My mind and body were falling apart, with them went my spirit.

I became confused and angry—at myself, at people I had trusted, and at God. I was alone in my mind with nowhere to go. I was separated from *all that is*. It was the perfect storm for my true awakening.

> Faith includes noticing the mess, the emptiness and discomfort, and letting it be there until some light returns.
>
> —Anne Lamott

I Am Grateful for the Dark Night

It has taken time to sort out and to integrate this journey, and as I wrote this book I could clearly see how it was all for a divine purpose. I am truly blessed and grateful for the dark-night experience.

I have turned all of my teachers into the greatest gifts I've ever known, including the one to whom I gave all of my power—for without them, I would not be who and what I am today.

My heart is free. I am no longer critical of my past choices and I have no self-judgment, blame, or lack of responsibility for my creations. I now know, without a doubt, that my life story had to span these vast landscapes to evolve. I had to lose it all to gain the wisdom that was sitting inside of me the whole time. It's the ultimate paradox: what you most seek is right there within you.

The problems, challenges, and deep, dark, devilish hardships we experience are a part of our unique story of transformation and soul growth. Life happens for us, not to us. We are the authors and we are the readers. Life is a messy, wild ride and it is our own personal creative co-creation.

No two souls' journeys are the same; that's why when you think about passing judgment on another, it's nearly impossible for that to make sense, as everyone has their personal ticket to their adventure on planet earth.

This book is certainly not my whole story. There is another book that will tell it all, but for now this book reflects the essence of my blues to bliss journey, and my desire is that it will assist you on yours.

What This Book *IS* and What It Isn't

This book was written for the consciously awakening human being who seeks uncomplicated practices for dedicated personal evolution. It's all about taking spiritual thought and putting it into practice.

This book does not advocate any one belief system, religious doctrine, or spiritual practice, but rather aims to simply express the divine nature of human existence through the lens that all things are living aspects of God and are governed by ageless universal laws.

As with every creative endeavor, magic happens when one is in flow with the universe. This book was a personal journey from thinking to feeling, doing to being, effort to allowing. There were times while writing when I closed my eyes and let my fingers type freely. When I reviewed what had been written, I often shed tears of joy. I knew that I was living my divine purpose and this was just the beginning of a new phase of my life story.

Throughout this book you will find the use of the words Universe, Source, Universal Force, Supreme Source, and Loving Creator. All these words are used to express the one Supreme Being: God.

By all means choose your own personal word for God. Try not to get attached to my chosen word, but rather the idea of the all-knowing and all-loving intelligence of the universe, of which you are made.

How This Book Can Lift You Up

As I began to do my own selected practices, I began to change, to *lighten up*. As you begin to use the practices, if you are open and ready, this divine light will flow through you and your experience as well.

Each time you use this book, ask intentionally for the most graceful experience of the highest intent to fulfill your practice. Then be ready to receive. You will go through your experiences, your wisdom will expand, and you will come to know who you truly are.

There is no time to wait. Open the book to any one of the 80 mindful practices and dive in. If you commit to the practices your life will shift. A lighter life is waiting, and I promise *bliss* is within reach.

How to Get the Most from This Book

The path that one person follows is not the correct path for any other person. Each of us must walk his own path to enlightenment—that is the way.

—Wu Wei

Pick Practices That Suit You

There are 80 practices, drawn from my personal spiritual journey and shared with you. They are meant to be *light-hearted, simple,* and *doable.* They are not meant to be deeply philosophical ideas. Not all of them will speak to you; pick the ones that do and leave the rest behind.

Each practice is numbered individually from 1 to 80. Following number 80 I've included a section titled *Your Mindful Practices.* This section will help you create a plan and to identify some specific habits that will make your practice a success.

Trust Your Intuition and Just Open and Read

The book is not designed to be read in sequential order. It's designed to be opened intuitively, to the practice that fits your needs in that moment. When you pick the book up ask, "Which practice is the best fit for what I need right now?" Then open the book and read what it says. If the practice feels like a fit, make it a part of your daily practice for as long as you feel you need it.

Or Use the Table of Contents

You can also use the *Table of Contents* to see if any words, titles, or themes pop out or feel in alignment with your needs for that day.

Match the Practice to Your Energy

Some practices are more involved than others, so pick the practices that you will commit to and do. Match the practice to your energy. Sometimes we need an easier practice and sometimes we feel like doing deeper or more committed work. Follow your energy. Trust yourself.

The Magic of Affirmations

Throughout the entire book, and included with each of the 80 practices, you will find an affirmation. These affirmations are the key to your transformation. Write them out, paste them on your mirror, kitchen cabinet, refrigerator, desk, nightstand, or wherever you frequently focus. Make them your consistent focus for the duration of your practice on a particular theme. Affirmations are powerful, especially when they begin with "I AM." Learn more about the use of conscious language in practice number 56, *Conscious Words*.

Why 80?

You may be wondering why there are 80 individual mindful practices. Numerology is important to me, as numbers are vibration. As I settled in to the intention behind this book, I ran across this perfect, descriptive meaning of the number 80. According to Joanne Walmsley of *Sacred Scribes* website,

> The number 8 brings inner-wisdom, personal authority, manifesting positive abundance and prosperity, success and achievement, dependability and stability, integrity and discernment, good judgment and problems-solving, and the concept of karma; the Universal Spiritual Law of Cause and Effect.
>
> The number 0 relates to the "God force" energy and eternity, continuing cycles and flow, and the beginning point. The number 0 resonates with potential and/or choice and relates to developing one's spiritual aspects as it is considered to represent the beginning of a spiritual journey and highlights the uncertainties that may entail.
>
> Angel number 80 brings a message from the angels that you are to use your personal power, tenacity and intelligence to achieve the successes you desire in your life. We create our own realities, and the angels want you to know that you have all the required skills, talents and abilities to achieve your desired results. ...Angel Number 80 suggests that you live your life with truth, honour and integrity, and make the most of your rewards and be grateful for your blessings.

That sounds good to me! Are you ready to dive in?

The Power of Your Heart

When human beings no longer think in matter,
but in the spirit, the heart will be the
organ of thinking.

—Rudolph Steiner

Understanding more about the heart has been a personal quest of mine. From spiritual experiences to scientific research, I have explored the power that the heart wields every day, all day long. It is said that the heart is the other brain in the body. When we make decisions through the heart, our decisions are aligned to our higher selves, our higher good. The heart is the organ in the body that has an intelligence greater than our ego mind and is the doorway to the divine.

In this book I often refer to "sitting in the heart." This means placing your focus on the heart region of your chest. Imagine yourself sitting, floating in your heart. As you sit there, focus on the sensations that inform your current state of being. Begin to focus on a loving memory and the feelings that accompany this memory.

Feel your heart begin to open. If you're not familiar with this practice, it may feel like your heart is cracking open. Opening the heart with love is a simple practice that leads to bliss; but first you may need to heal some things, or remove some blocks to clear the way.

(For instructions on Sitting in the Heart, turn to the section titled *Quick Access Practices*.)

Blues and the Array of Emotions

Feeling blue or even mildly depressed can make your heart feel heavy, as if an anvil were sitting on your chest. It can cause your chest to feel compressed or constricted. It can feel nearly impossible to lift the heaviness.

The good news is that it is possible to move yourself from this deep, lower vibration and emotion to more light. Everyone is different and this does not imply clinical depression, rather what we know as *the blues*. Moving from the blues toward bliss happens one step at a time, in increments of joy and baby steps toward the light.

In this book, you will learn about the vibrational scale of emotion and how to move from the blues to more joy and bliss.

The Truth of Bliss

Having experienced bliss, I still can barely put words to it. This experience was so vast and so fulfilling that I just wanted to stay still. I felt that if I moved it would disappear. In truth, it sits waiting inside each of us at all times.

Bliss is like white light. Just as pure light is the totality of all color, bliss is the conglomeration of all positive qualities. When seen through the prism of spiritual awareness, the subcomponents of bliss are joy, unconditional love, inner peace, power, connectedness, awe, and wisdom. Bliss cannot even be attained, really. The soul simply realizes that bliss simply is. It is what remains after everything external and fleeting disappears.

—Sean Meshorer

Bliss simply is, and it's the unwrapping of the prison we put around us that keeps it from the surface of our experience. It's comforting to know that we can *be* it at any time.

The Practice of Love

I'm going to share a secret, right out of the gate. I'm going to tell you how I experienced bliss. I want you to know that this experience is waiting for you, or maybe you've experienced it and are trying to get back there. The answers reside in the power of your heart.

Here's my story....

I had been doing quite a bit of work to heal my stories and free myself from suffering, and my spiritual teacher had been doing some deep work on my energy to open my heart. I found myself traveling with some dear friends, attending a personal development workshop. At this event there were many opportunities to hold my heart open in non-judgment and love. I even managed to let my ego flare up in an argument with someone. I quickly claimed the lesson and got into my heart. As I focused on love in my heart, it began to widen, as if it were literally one with everything.

Tears rolled freely down my cheeks. As this experience continued I found myself in a state of serenity like I had never experienced before. I focused on keeping my heart open in all experiences for the next few days. It was clear to me that my ego had taken a back seat and my heart was driving. There was nothing to do, but just *be*. I was experiencing being in the world, but not of it. I stayed in this place by simply focusing on holding my heart open and being love. No matter what anyone else did or said, or what was going on in the world, I was the same. I was in bliss.

My profound lesson was that the art of being love means having no agenda, no expected outcomes, no judgment, nothing but an open feeling of acceptance. Everything that *IS*, just is. There is nothing to *DO*. It's in the *being* that you become a conduit for the highest vibration on earth: love.

Miracle Mindset

You have noticed that everything an Indian does is in a circle, and that is because the Power of the World always works in circles, and everything tries to be round. The Sky is round, and I have heard that the earth is round like a ball, and so are all the stars. The wind, in its greatest power, whirls. Birds make their nest in circles, for theirs is the same religion as ours....

Even the seasons form a great circle in their changing, and always come back again to where they were. The life of a human is a circle from childhood to childhood, and so it is in everything where power moves.

—Black Elk

Around and 'Round We Go

It helps to put life's cycles into reasoning. If you ascribe to the idea that we are spiritual beings having a human experience, then the journey is the unfolding and learning of all that is human—especially the world of emotions. We attract or manifest experiences so that we can remember our way back to our highest selves. This journey is bumpy and filled with manholes and mountains but, the truth is, everything is already in perfect order—we are just finding our way to that truth.

This first section provides various perspectives and practices for you to consider if you feel lost, confused, or dismayed by the stage of life you may find yourself experiencing. The natural rules of transformation make sense out of seemingly senseless change. Some of us must travel to the depths of despair to seize the true light. This is the mystery of the human journey, and no one escapes the path.

Remember, you are in charge of your perceptions and choices. You have the power to choose your mindset at any given moment. You have the power to see truth. And you have ability to use your superpowers to shift your life. *That is the big secret.* There, now you know.

You are in the right place.

1

The Nature of Transformation

Our ego mind would love to think that we can slow the spin of the planet and the myriad of changes that take hold in our lives every day. From the moment we are born we begin a process of transformation. Nothing stays the same, not even our cells from one moment to the next.

If transformation is a given in our human lives, how do we embrace it rather than resist or fight it? William Bridges, one of my favorite authors, wrote in his book *Transitions* that "in order for there to be a new beginning, there must be an ending, and in the middle is the neutral zone." Let's review this:

1. THE BEGINNING - Once you choose a new beginning, you put thoughts and emotions in play which then trigger a shift. This trigger unfolds a new reality of your creation. You are in charge. By choosing consciously, you create your life. Thoughts with no conscious choice create a life of happenstance. *The trick is to choose consciously.* What do you want?

2. THE ENDING - You must let go of events from the past to create room for the potential of what you want. Letting go means releasing thoughts, emotions, intentions, memories, agreements, and contracts that no longer serve you. *Letting go means to let it fade away; be done with it.*

3. THE NEUTRAL ZONE - Then there's the neutral zone, the place that can be most uncomfortable, the letting go of the outcome, the I-don't-know zone, the I-don't-have-a-clue zone. The time frame for this stage is unknown. You'll know that

you're in the neutral zone when you don't have the answers or know the outcomes.

Transformation happens. Change happens. Creation happens. The question is, are you consciously creating or unconsciously manifesting?

Get comfortable with change, make it conscious and feel the power to create the life you want.

Affirmation:
I am conscious of my choices. I create what I desire.

Everyone wants to transform, but nobody wants to change.

—Frederica Mathewes-Green

2

Seasons and Cycles to Life

There are seasons and cycles—winter, spring, summer, fall. The natural seasons don't necessarily correlate to the seasons you experience in life. Sometimes you feel like hibernating in the summer or feel active in the winter. It's natural and appropriate to follow your own rhythms.

What season are you in?

- **Winter** - time to go inward, to contemplate, to reflect, to restore

- **Spring** - time to clear out, spring forward, create, bring fresh ideas into the light

- **Summer** - time to play, enjoy, be with friends and family, adventure out, travel

- **Fall** - time to slow down, let go, release, shed, stock up, collect the harvest

Maybe you're on the cusp of a season. Maybe your inner season is in sync with nature. How do you feel?

You can use the energy of the seasons to make changes, to reflect, and to gather your resources. The energy of spring can inspire waking up, clearing out, and refreshing your life; it can also feel like reflecting on your options and making a new plan. The energy of winter can motivate you to simplify, and the energy of fall can aid you in unwinding.

Honor your season and your rhythm and feel in flow.

There are seasons in life. Don't ever let anyone try to deny you the joy of one season because they believe you should stay in another season.... Listen to yourself. Trust your instincts.
Keep your perspective.

—Jane Clayso

3

When You've Lost Your Passion

The ebb and flow of life brings us in and out of alignment with our passion. We can use this natural occurrence to our advantage. It can be a time to check in and test whether or not something you've been doing is a passion or just another thing you're doing.

If you feel flat or a bit depressed, take it as sign that you have lost touch with what strums your soul. To live in your passion is to feel connected to your true work, a hobby, or volunteer activity, and to be in sync with your heart.

Being out of passion means you've sacrificed your unique gift in exchange for something else. You may even know what it is. Maybe you believe you're not deserving, or that you can't afford it, or that it has to be a side job.

Many people don't know their passion; but every person has a cause living within. My dear friend Gregg Levoy, in his book *Vital Signs*, says "...you can cultivate not just a specific passion, but passion as a mind-set—a stance—that helps bring vitality to all your engagements, from work and relationships to creativity and spiritual life."

There seems to be an underlying belief in our culture that living your passion is selfish. This is a myth. Finding your passion means breaking through fears, taking risks, and going against the naysayers and opinions of family, friends, and society.

Living your passion is living your God-given essence. It's living in alignment with a truth so powerful that when you align with it, everything falls into place. It means standing in your authentic power.

40

Find Your Passion

Start here to get back in alignment with your purpose, your passion, and your synchronicity with life:

- Stop everything you're doing, sit down, breathe in, and sink into your heart.

- Sit and listen to what comes.

- After a few moments ask, "What shall I focus on that brings me joy?" Listen until your answer comes.

When I recently asked this I heard, "Laugh." How simple is that? I needed to laugh to begin the journey back to my passion. Your heart always knows. Take the time to sit, breathe, and ask. Then listen.

Once you're in a greater state of joy, start asking harder questions:

- What is my passion?

- What am I to do in this world that fills my heart and brings me joy?

- What makes me happy when I do it?

- What makes me go timeless?

- What just feels right when I spend time dedicated to it?

Skip the how-do-I-make-money question. Dream, become expansive, and fill your heart up with what brings you pleasure. This is where you lift yourself from lost to found. It's a start!

Affirmation:
I am living my passion now and in every moment.

We can find passion in what we do but it cannot be found in what you detest doing.

—Byron Pulsifer

You are held.

4

You're Never Alone

It can appear that we are separate, alone, going solo. This is not true. We are connected to everything and it's all moving in unison with everything else. You are a part of the whole. Without you, the world would miss your unique contribution that only you can make. It matters. It all matters!

You are connected to those with whom you work, clients, family, and even to the barista at your favorite coffee house. As you experience your day, with all of these people moving about, you realize that you are connected to them and they to you. Stop and observe how elegant the universe truly is.

Connect to the Whole and See Your Part

As a part of this magnificent wholeness, you have the power to create a wave of positivity or a tsunami of frustration. If you choose in your day to see peace, you will find that peace builds inside of you. This is how the whole reflects back. Try it and see what happens. Be peace for an entire day. Smile, nod, compliment others, and listen. Watch what happens to the energy around you. You will never feel alone again.

Affirmation:
I am a part of the whole, and my part makes a difference.

You are never alone, you are eternally connected
to everything and everyone.

—Amit Ray

5

Stepping Through the Veil of Illusion

Making changes in our lives can seem daunting. We wake up and start our day with the best of intentions, then find ourselves following a similar pattern or a habitual set of actions. Changing our ways is as simple as stepping through the veil of illusion.

Imagine a sheer curtain separating you from your desired life. All you have to do is take your hand and gently pull it back to reveal your new world, your new way of being, your new life. It really is that easy.

The veil is created by old thoughts, thoughts imprinted by past experiences. If we just decide to abandon our thoughts, take a breath, and step forward into a new reality, we will find that we are standing in our new truth and that life has forever changed. We will look back and say, "That wasn't so hard!"

Just Step

Here are the keys to stepping through the veil of illusion:

- Decide that you want to move forward.

- Breathe deeply.

- Get into your heart space.

- Step without thinking; just step.

Try this with something you've wanted to change. Once you do it you will do it again and again to get the same result. This is the secret to opening to a life filled with joy and ease, and free from fear.

Affirmation:
I am awake and I am stepping into my dream with joy and ease.

A life truly lived constantly burns away the veils of illusion, burns away what is no longer relevant, until, at last, we are strong enough to stand in our naked truth.

—Marion Woodman

6

Perspective Can Make or Break You

How you experience your day is a matter of perspective. Perspective is based on your beliefs, and beliefs can be steadfast. But your beliefs can also be changeable—even deletable.

Change Your Perspective

Observe your perspectives and your beliefs without judgment. View yourself as though you were watching through a pane of glass. Keep a journal of the beliefs you notice. At the end of the day review and assess each one. Does the belief

- serve you in a positive way,

- serve you in a negative way,

- inspire you or keep you in a pattern?

Once you've reviewed your thoughts, consider the following:

- Perspectives are based on your life experiences and can change. Which perspectives from this exercise would you like to change?

- You are solely accountable for your beliefs. Are there any beliefs that you would like to let go of, shift, or define even further?

- Talk to others about your perspectives and see if they have ideas that may help you shift yours.

Perspectives keep our lives in a specific order. Do you need to shake it up? Do you need to change your perspectives to shift your life? These are good questions to ask yourself each day.

Affirmation:

I am willing to observe my perspectives and shift those that no longer serve me.

We can complain because rose bushes have thorns, or rejoice because thorn bushes have roses.

—Abraham Lincoln

7

The Matter of Abundance

When contemplating abundance we often think of wealth or money. It's so much more than that. The dictionary defines abundance as a very large quantity of something, or more than enough. The truth is that the universe is unlimited, infinite. It's the human mind that puts limitations on something that is constantly expanding and evolving.

In their book *Creating Money: Attracting Abundance*, Sanaya Roman and Duane Packer state,

> You are the source of your riches, not your job, your investments, your spouse, or your parents. By linking with the unlimited abundance of your soul or higher self, by opening your connection to the higher forces ... by expressing and radiating your higher qualities of inner peace, joy, love, well-being, and aliveness, you become the source of your abundance.

This entire book is designed to help you open the gates to what's already there—as everything you desire already exists. Open your mind, open your heart, and get in sync with natural law. It's more simple than you think.

Open Your Mind

Take a moment and look around you, especially at nature. What do you see? Nature is in perfect order, ebbing and flowing, creating and decaying, birthing and dying. It is in constant birth and rebirth. Allow your mind to truly see the abundance all around you. And then turn on your heart with gratitude—more gratitude and more until you feel your heart want to crack open.

This is abundance and you have the power within you to create anything you desire.

Affirmation:
I am in complete abundance at all times.

I live in an abundant universe.
I always have everything I need.

—Sanya Roman, Duane Packer

8

Following Your Natural Rhythm

Do you follow your energetic state or do you override it? There is a natural flow to our biology, just as there is a natural flow to the seasons of nature. In our busy world we tend to override our natural state to get things done. With the additional communication devices there really is no place to unhook from the constant barrage of information, task lists, and obligations.

Try to follow your natural flow. If you need a little extra sleep, make an effort to get it. If you need some quiet time, find it—even if it's just for ten minutes. If you need some focused time to accomplish something, create the environment to do so. If you need stimulation, connect with someone.

Following your natural rhythm—even a little bit—helps you to feel more grounded. In doing so you honor yourself and your body.

Honor your natural rhythm to the best of your ability. When you force yourself into unnatural energy outputs, you will eventually become drained. Breathing always helps!

Affirmation:
I honor my natural energy rhythms.

When you are in vibrational harmony, your body produces whatever it needs to remain in perfect balance.

—Abraham-Hicks

9

Mastering Feelings and Emotions

You are in charge. You have the capacity to determine the way you feel. Your thoughts and beliefs cause your feelings and emotions. You can change what you think and alter your feelings and emotions. Shift your thoughts and you shift your reality. Once you disassociate with your negative ego and create awareness of your subconscious mind, you can begin to trust your feelings and emotions.

One way to move forward is to release your emotions in a healthy, expressive manner, like hitting a pillow or dancing wildly. If you stuff your emotions, it can create a buildup of negative energy. This can make you sick. Living in a continuous state of suppression can literally kill you!

In order to heal and grow into self-mastery, we need to integrate all of the parts of ourselves in order. The masculine, feminine, inner child, and the goddess are all parts of who we are. If the negative ego runs the show we continually loop around old, familiar lessons. If the conscious-self leads the way, we learn and grow with more accountability and less struggle.

Heal Those Emotions

Identify which feelings and emotions repeatedly come to the surface. Which ones on this list look familiar to you? Be honest with yourself.

Shame, guilt, blame, despair, regret, grief, fear, anxiety, aggression, resentment, hopelessness, betrayal, failure, hatred, perfectionism, greed, compulsiveness, violation, survival, anger, apathy, misery, disgust, lack of trust, self-pity, envy, competition, disdain, sadness, rejection, suspicion,

54

melancholy, depression, boredom, scared, aggravation, humiliation, neglect, exasperation.

There are many ways to approach personal healing. The first step is to *become aware* of which emotions you want to understand, integrate, release, and heal. Commit to a healing method that works for you. It is a process and it is a conscious choice to begin.

Affirmation:
I am expressing my feelings and emotions in a healthy way.
I am releasing negative emotions and I am healing now.

There are only two emotions, love and fear.
Chose whom ye shall serve.

—A Course in Miracles

10

Understanding the Mirror

There is a cause and effect, action and reaction in the universe. It's inevitable. Some call it karma, others describe it as a given dynamic. For everything there is a direct reflection of like kind.

We reap what we sow.

To become more conscious of the reality you are manifesting, you need to know about your subconscious patterns, your triggers, and wounds. This will reveal the unconscious psychological aspects that currently create your world.

If you ascribe to this universal law, then you realize every choice you make creates a response. Every action creates a reaction. This is where personal *respons-ability* comes in. If you choose to be a conscious being, it becomes your responsibility to claim this power and demonstrate your highest self with every thought, feeling, and emotion.

It means leaving victimhood behind and accepting responsibility for your entire life force. It also means that the results in your life are yours only and not based on others. Your focus must be turned completely upon yourself as the creator of your reality. It is a discipline that requires 100% commitment. This can be an outright daunting task. The reward, however, is that you deeply understand the mirror, your responsibility to yourself, and begin to live as if everything you think, say, and do matters.

Your Body Knows

You're living in the best tool there is for making conscious choices—your body. It has the intelligence to help you discern what aligns with your higher self. As you learn to read your body, you will discover that your feelings tell you when a choice is unfit, and when it is right for you. If you check in with your heart, it will give you the true answer. Know that sometimes we make decisions so that we can learn.

Here's how to check in with your body and your heart:

- Sit quietly and be still.

- Breathe deeply to clear any distress.

- Imagine in your mind the choice you're about to make.

- Focus on your body and feel what feels joyful versus uneasy.

- Ask your heart, "Is this choice in my best interest?"

- Listen and feel the answer. Let your body and your heart tell you.

- Trust your insights.

How many times have you heard yourself say, "I knew the right decision, and I didn't listen to myself."

Look clearly and honestly at the mirror of your life. Take full responsibility for your life force. Become a conscious choice-maker and watch what happens!

Affirmation:
I take 100% responsibility for my choices.

Life is a Mirror which you created in order to be able to see all of the conscious and unconscious beliefs which are running you. You did this in order to be able to gain control over your life by changing this unconsciously learned behaviour so that you might evolve and grow as a Human Being.

—Anunda, Lifestreams

Everything is a vibration, everything.

11

Raising Your Vibration

The human condition creates for you a myriad of emotions throughout your day. These emotions are actually vibrations. As you emote, you send a vibrational signal into the fabric of the universe. The universe then matches that vibration and sends your creation back to you. You've heard that like attracts like. Well, yes it does.

David Hawkins wrote a book in 2002 titled *Power vs. Force: The Hidden Determinants of Human Behavior*. This book appeared at the forefront of our understanding of how emotions create vibrations. What I find most intriguing about this book is Hawkins' Map of Consciousness. The map shows the scale of emotions and their vibrational equivalents. One can test vibrational levels through the use of kinesiology or muscle testing. The scale ranges from 20 to 1,000. The highest 300 points of the scale represent an indescribable or enlightened emotion. The bottom of the scale relates to the emotion of humiliation (shame). As you can see, there are various emotions in between. Abraham-Hicks and other experts have revealed this type of emotional chart and method of seeing, indicating that we may be vibrating when experiencing an emotional state.

The goal, of course, is to try to raise our vibration—allowing us to live in a greater state of joy (or 540 on the scale, which correlates to a very-high vibration). At a minimum, we can strive for 250, which is the emotion of trust (neutrality). Here is a basic representation of the scale:

700 – 1,000	Indescribable (enlightenment)
600	Bliss (Peace)
540	Serenity (Joy)
500	Reverence (Love)
400	Understanding (Reason)
350	Forgiveness (Acceptance)
310	Optimism (Willingness)
250	Trust (Neutrality)
200	Affirmation (Courage)
175	Scorn (Pride)
150	Hate (Anger)
125	Craving (Desire)
100	Anxiety (Fear)
75	Regret (Grief)
50	Despair (Apathy)
30	Blame (Guilt)
20	Humiliation (Shame)

Use your body as a kinesthetic-feedback tool to determine where you are vibrating. Here's how:

1. Stand, feet firmly on the floor. Close your eyes and ask your body to show you a YES. Let your body move in the direction it naturally wants to go. In many cases your body will fall forward for a YES.

2. Next, with your eyes closed, ask your body to show you a NO. Your body may fall backward. Whatever direction your body falls is your own internal compass for your NO.

3. To determine your vibration level, ask this yes-no question: "Using the Map of Consciousness, is my vibrational level above a 20?" Give your body time to

fall in its natural direction. Continue moving up the scale until you reach a NO. Then you will know which general vibrational level you are at presently.

Note: Your mind can alter the outcomes of this method if you let your ego get in the way. Stay unattached to the outcome and set an intention to know the truth.

Try to raise your vibration at least one level, if not more, at one time. Do this by focusing on a memory that resonates with that particular emotion. For instance, to move from shame to grief, allow yourself to cry, release, and let go. Then test your vibrational level again to see if you've moved up on the vibrational scale.

Move up as many emotional levels as you authentically can. You'll notice that if you can get yourself up to 250 you are at neutrality. This is a great goal if you're living in the lower vibrations. Sometimes it just takes one step toward a higher vibration to start the ball rolling.

Notice that when you're in the lower vibrational frequencies you attract others who are also vibrating at those frequencies. When you're feeling poorly it's best to connect with beings who are vibrating at higher levels.

Affirmation:
I am raising my vibration now, one step at a time.

Hold the space, shine the light, raise the global vibration ever closer to the frequency of our Loving Creator. That's why we're on the planet.

—Dana Taylor

12

Holding Your Frequency

Life is a swirl of energy—rising, dropping, weaving, and bobbing. In the center of all the chaos there is a place of stillness and calm—like the eye of a tornado. It's natural law.

As a spiritual being having a human experience, with a body full of emotions, it can be challenging to find the calm center and a sense of balance. Yet we are called to this mastery every minute of every day. As fellow humans on an evolutionary path, we seek to find the unshakeable place where we stand in our personal power.

Achieving mastery in holding your frequency is a tall order, especially considering cultural conditioning and your unique emotional landscape. Mastery relies on many of the skills explained in this book. Integrate your whole self, leave past conditioning behind, and embrace a new way of being human. This is our divine destiny.

Here are some tips for *holding your frequency*:

1. Know that *you are in control* of your state of being. The world isn't happening to you; you are happening to it.

2. Know that other people's emotions are not yours, and that other people have the right to feel whatever they need to feel in their experience. You do not have to react or even respond to someone else's emotions. Hold still with compassion.

3. Get into your heart by focusing on something you love, and feel your heart open. Open it wider and wider and wider. Hold your heart open while

witnessing an intense situation. Be still; be in your heart.

4. Hold the energy of neutrality and do not attach to someone else's emotional journey.

5. Witness without judgment, but with compassion.

Affirmation:
I am compassionate, neutral, and a non-reactive witness.

Everything begins to change once you begin emitting your own frequency instead of absorbing the frequencies around you.

—Tiffany Stiles

13

Aligning Energy

What does it mean to *align energy*? In my universe, it means to be conscious of your feelings, emotions, and state of being, and how that impacts your desired outcomes. When you are out of alignment, you are what I call *off the rails*. This means that the outcomes you seek have no chance of coming to fruition because you are out of sync and misaligned to your goals.

When your energy is aligned and in sync, you feel a state of flow, synchronicity, and ease. This is a state of *being*, not forcing or doing. Struggles fade, joy returns, and a high vibrational energy becomes your predominant way of being.

A clear personal vision (intent) aligned to your natural energy is the optimal condition for successful fulfillment. Passion, focus, and action contribute to the results you seek. You are aligned.

Alignment Equals Flow

How to align your energy:

1. Start by seeing honestly and clearly what exists in your life now (the mirror).

2. Look at everything in your life and ask, "Is this in or out of alignment with where I am right now?" That question can be applied to projects, goals, how you spend your time, people in your life, clients in your business, and how you choose to spend your life.

3. Then, eliminate unnecessary things—projects, relationships, ways of spending time, expired commitments, obligations, etc. Be ruthless with this

activity and you will experience a release of the things that presently drain you and cloud your joy.

4. Align by creating a clear, meaningful, and purposeful vision for what's next in your life. Then let the natural flow of energy show you the way. Follow clues. Watch for synchronicities. Say yes to what feels in-flow, and no to what feels out of sync.

How often do you have to reassess if your energy is aligned or not? In every situation, all day long. Use your intuition to advise you of things that feel in alignment or not. Use your gut to tell you if it feels good to you or off. Check in.

Affirmation:
I am aligned in my energy and purpose with everything in my life.

The universe does not know whether the vibration that you're offering is because of something you're observing or something you're remembering or something that you are imagining. It just receives the vibration and answers it with things that match it.

—Abraham-Hicks

14

Self-Leadership and Personal Power

The more dedicated you are to take responsibility for 100% of your life force, your choices, and your way of being, the more likely you are to open the door to enlightenment.

Self-leadership is the choice that puts you in the driver's seat of your experiences, your relationships, and your own evolution. It is the decision to be accountable to how your life force interacts within and with the world. As a spiritually responsible person, you devote your mindset to practicing the universal laws that lead to alignment with your highest truth and purpose.

You strengthen the magnitude of your personal power by being diligent with your conscious choices. Strong leaders maintain their personal power at all times. Dr. Joshua David Stone, a spiritual teacher, shared that "...a sovereign leader is as tough as nails in her focus and discipline, but as loving and harmless as the Virgin Mary."

You never give your personal power away to anyone or anything, including your own runaway thoughts, feelings, emotions, appetites, and other ego-driven desires. You have this much power. Have you accepted this, or are you still allowing others to dictate how you should think and feel?

When I dropped into my dark night of the soul experience, I lost grasp of this knowing. There are many reasons we go through such an experience. In my case, it was about learning not to give my power away, letting go of victim mentality, understanding the true nature of faith, and taking 100% responsibility for my life force. This experience hit me like a truck and dropped me to my knees. I came apart and was faced with one choice: surrender.

As I waded through the dark landscape, facing my ego, my mistakes, failures, trespasses, critical self-judgment, shame, guilt, grief, and the truth of my creations, I got it—it's all mine and I have the power to change it and rise again. This was the most powerful moment in my life.

As a result, I became increasingly more sovereign and began the journey of cleaning up my messes. Sovereignty is freedom from the influence of others; it's then just you and your relationship with your Loving Creator. It's a place of *being* that is governed by owning the outcomes of every experience and thought, of *being* and acting under your sovereign guidance system.

You realize that you do not have control over others, just yourself. You are sovereign and free to align with higher intelligence.

Affirmation:
I am sovereign in my way of being and leading.

A sovereign being is one who has broken free of culture's conditioning, referring to a higher wisdom from within that serves the good of all. This is where your true freedom awaits you. It requires your full presence. One can no longer play the victim in this space. Instead, one becomes a leader.

——Christine Horner

15

Clearing Out

It's time to clear some things out. Look around and identify something in your home or office that is weighing you down or that you're avoiding.

If you had an energy meter that measured energy on a scale from one to ten (ten being a lot of energy, one being very little), where does that item you found land on the scale? How much energy is it taking?

Let Go

Free up some energy by letting go of something you no longer need. Here are some ideas of things to let go of:

- A pile of paper in your home or office
- A pile of little things on your countertop
- The contents of a drawer, bin, or box
- Items on a shelf in a closet
- Things collecting in the console of your car
- An item that holds negative energy from the past
- An item that you no longer use
- An item that is no longer beautiful to you

Just let one of these things go. Even just a little bit of clearing and letting go will free up some energy. Do it now.

Affirmation:
I am clearing the way for new energy.

Ask yourself who you want to be and what you want to do. If a thing does not inspire or serve that purpose, it goes.

—Evan Zislis

On Being You

If knowing yourself and being yourself were as easy to do as to talk about, there wouldn't be nearly so many people walking around in borrowed postures, spouting secondhand ideas, trying desperately to fit in rather than to stand out.

—Warren G. Bennis

It Takes Great Courage to Be Your Authentic Self

It requires wild abandon of constraints you may perceive in the world. You must shake off what others think of you—their opinions, advice, and input. You must cut free!

There's nothing like meeting a person who embodies her authenticity in full bloom. Can you think of someone you know who lives in alignment with that inner truth? How would you describe that person? What traits do you admire? Guess what? Those traits are also in you or you wouldn't be able to see them.

There is only one you with your unique creative expression. Who are you? The world needs you now.

You are an original.

16

Your Life on Purpose

It is a rigorous journey to determine your perception of your purpose in this life. It's a human trait to search for meaning. Your purpose can remain an eternal mystery, or it can become an experience in joyful, creative expression of your highest self.

What if you started the journey with the belief that you are truly unique and alive to fulfill a divine purpose, as an expression of Source?

Mining this truth can begin with identifying what you do more uniquely than others. When you then match your uniqueness to a need in the world you experience synchronicity and flow.

If you spend your time trying to *DO* things you are skilled at, but that are not necessarily your unique, divine talents, you create a misalignment in your energy. This effort, if truly out of sync, will begin to drain you, frustrate you, and turn your reality into a struggle. Often, this disconnect is fueled by survival. How will I make money? How will I survive? How will I live my dreams and achieve my goals?

When I'm Timeless

Discover your life on purpose:

1. Ask yourself this, "What does it feel like when I'm timeless, in joy, and loving what I'm doing?" Make a list of all of these things.

2. Where do you spend your time focusing? On what?

3. Make a list of the richest life lessons you've had to learn. Many times our own story becomes exactly

how we can then help others. This can include core personal wounds, mistakes, failures, and experiences that transformed you.

4. Determine who in the world has a need for your unique gifts. Why do they have that need? What are their problems, pains, or struggles that your talent can resolve? Where does your life meet theirs? Where does your wisdom meet their deep need?

The answer to living a life on purpose is within this list. If it's not one thing, it may be a creative combination of things.

After you complete this exercise, create a clear vision. Your clarity, commitment, and discipline to living your purpose will easily make it a reality.

Affirmation:
I am living my life on purpose and in alignment with my divine gifts. I am in service to the higher good of humanity.

Start embracing the life that is calling you. Find your calling. Know what sparks the light in you so—in your own way—can illuminate the world.

—Oprah Winfrey

17

Dance Naked in Your Authenticity

It would be nice if we could just be who we truly are. Authenticity is the act of being truthful with yourself and others. It means that you are clear on who you are, and that you stand with strength in your own shoes.

Choosing authenticity means cultivating the courage to be emotionally honest, to set boundaries, and to allow ourselves to be vulnerable; exercising the compassion that comes from knowing that we are all made of strength and struggle and connected to each other through loving and resilient human spirit; nurturing the connection and sense of belonging that can only happen when we let go of what we are supposed to be and embrace who we are.

——Brené Brown

The easiest way to just be, is to sit in the heart and let go of everything around you except for the joyous feeling you feel deep inside at the center of your being—the one that feels good, that feels true, that has no agenda, sees no right or wrong, and is just simply being the love that you are.

Live fully. Be fully. Open your heart. Laugh. Sing. Dance. Write poetry. Skip rocks. Light a sparkler. Breathe in the fresh, beautiful air—the molecules of life itself.

Affirmation:
I am authentically me; I can just be.

The authentic self is soul made visible.

—Sarah Ban Breathnach

18

You Are Enough

Much of the time we are drawn into the mindset that we're not enough, that we're not doing enough, or that we're missing something. We may compete with others, ourselves, or our ego's list of shoulds. This is just a reminder that you already are everything you need to be, just as you are, right here and right now.

You are perfect. There's no need to try to become anything else; just expressing who you are is a gift to the world. Feeling the joy inside your own heart and loving yourself are the only things to hold in your focus. If you do this, partnered with your creativity and your clear intentions and desires, the rest will take care of itself.

Keep it simple. Keep it light. Keep loving yourself for all that you are and the world will show you more of exactly that.

Affirmation:
I am perfection.

Love yourself first and everything else falls into line. You really have to love yourself to get anything done in this world.

—Lucille Ball

You are pure love.

19

Let Loose with Self-Love

Do you find it hard to put on and take off those various masks you wear when you're with clients or co-workers? What if you could just be you today, all of you? What would that look like? Are you giggling or gasping as you entertain that idea?

Being who you are is sometimes perceived as risky. If you show up as who you really are, you might be criticized, shamed, ignored, or, worse, ridiculed. But what if you didn't care? What if being you and letting go of all outside expectations was easy? What if you let go of caring about being judged?

Okay, let go. Be you. Let loose. You might have more fun if you show up as yourself. You know when you're on an airplane and you start talking to the person next to you and you share intimate details of your life? It's like that.

Cut Loose

Have coffee or a meal with someone who doesn't know you very well and share your real you. Ask that person to share their authentic self, too. See what kind of friendship you can start by being who you really are. Show up. Share. Set yourself free.

Affirmation:
I am me, all of me, and I am loved.

Because true belonging only happens when we present our authentic, imperfect selves to the world, our sense of belonging can never be greater than our level of self-acceptance.

——Brené Brown

20

See Your Brilliance

Seeing yourself as brilliant may feel like a self-absorbed act, but it's actually the one thing we can do to align ourselves to the pure truth. Within you is the divine spark of God. You are brilliant without even trying.

When you see someone who sparkles, what is it that you're seeing? You're seeing a higher vibration energy and someone who is living from the heart. It's beautiful when you see and feel this energy in someone. They have an attraction factor that is magnetic and brilliant.

In renowned artist Glenda Green's book *Love Without End*, she describes Jesus Christ appearing to her for four months while she painted his portrait. During these conversations Jesus shared with Glenda the nature of adamantine particles. Green recounts,

> *"The sharing of adamantine particles is the breath of life,"* Jesus said. *"There is an ongoing exchange of these particles throughout existence. They not only comprise organic life, but also the planet, the wind, and every substance that is. Everything breathes for the whole of its duration. Inhaling and exhaling, these particles bring vital balance and connections to life.*
> *"Adamantine particles belong to both the infinite world and to the limited realm of physical existence. They were the 'First Light' of creation. They are forever the light of consciousness. They provide the fuel and the dynamic energy to propel thoughts into manifestation. They give flesh to spirit, as well as new life, beauty, nourishment, and healing to life. Because they are commanded by love and conform to the nature and will of spirit, adamantine particles belong to all dimensions."*

There is no limit to the number of these particles you can draw to you through the power of love. When we breathe and oxygenate our blood, the particles become embedded into our whole biology and radiate from every cell. The more we acknowledge and breathe in these particles, the more light we are capable of carrying.

Given this incredible description of what we are made of, the simple truth is that the more we become love in our hearts, the more brilliant we become—literally.

You are unquestionably brilliant, right down to your DNA. Your unique way of being in the world is one of a kind and this world would be very different without you in it.

If you have ever thought that you don't matter, now is the time to exterminate that belief and welcome the fact that you are perfect. You are magnificent in all ways. Every speck of you is blazing with divine perfection.

Believe, embrace, and shine your brilliance. Breathe in your greatness from the depths of your heart. Let your heart expand and let your breath fill your lungs with sparkling atoms of acceptance.

Allow yourself to be perfect, because you already are.

Affirmation:
I am complete perfection in all ways, as I am. I am brilliant.

You are a Divine creation, a Being of Light who showed up here as a human being at the exact moment you were supposed to. You are the Beloved, a miracle, a part of the eternal perfection.

—Dr. Wayne Dyer

Shine.

21

Claim Your Creative License

"Creativity is the natural order of life. Life is energy: pure creative energy," says Julia Cameron, author of *The Artist's Way*. "When we open ourselves to our creativity, we open ourselves to the Creator's creativity within us and our lives. Creativity is God's gift to us. Using our creativity is our gift back to God."

It's our divine right to express our uniqueness. There is only one of you. What one thing in your life, right now, is uniquely you? Maybe it's a perspective, a desire, a thought. Maybe it's a physical aspect, a belief you have, or a piece of wisdom. What do you want to express?

Creative license is a concept that gives you the right to express yourself in the highest light of who you are, in all your uniqueness.

Take one creative aspect of yourself and let it fly. Try it for a day. Once you do, notice how the world responds to you. I bet you'll inspire others to do the same.

Letting our creative, unique selves out to play causes joy to spawn in the world. Go ahead, be you, be free, be all that you can be today in your unique, amazing, special self.

Affirmation:
I am creative and allow the creative force to flow through me.

There is only one of you in all time, this expression is unique. And if you block it, it will never exist through any other medium and it will be lost.

—Martha Graham

Go Easy on Yourself

At the center of your being
you have the answer;
you know who you are
and you know what you want.

—Lao Tzu

Leave Your Inner Critic Behind

There are those who say, be hard on yourself so the rest of the world won't be harder on you than you are. As a self-proclaimed, harsh inner critic, I disagree. When you are hard on yourself, you lower your vibrational frequency and begin to attract to you that match. Rather, I suggest celebrating your strengths and creating practices to shift your perceived weaknesses.

Going easy on yourself means to be realistic about the view you have of yourself, and filling it with compassion and great self-love while you're being honest and mapping your growth. It means to trust your inner guidance and know that your mistakes and failures are opportunities for learning and change.

Be kind to yourself, celebrate your true value, and express that in the world. Then the world can reflect who you truly are.

Go high.

22

Stay out of the Rabbit Hole

Whenever you feel you haven't done something well or tried hard enough, you put yourself in a cycle of self-criticism and judgment. This then feeds your ego mind to say, "Aha! See? You will never succeed or become a success."

The energy of self-judgment draws you deep into a resonance of shame. The lower you go the more your ego mind feels justified in its beliefs. Your energy drains and soon you find yourself despising being in the world. If you go far enough down this rabbit hole you end up in depression.

Run, Rabbit, Run

Be easy on yourself by stopping the minute you hear and feel these negative thoughts come into your mind. Take three deep breaths. Drop into your heart by focusing on the center of your chest and thinking about something you love, then repeat the affirmation below.

Affirmation:
There is nothing I need to do to prove myself to anyone
and most certainly to myself.
I am loved. I am loved. I am loved and accepted for who I am.

The only person who can pull me down is myself,
and I'm not going to let myself pull me down
anymore.

—C. JoyBell C.

23

Be Compassion

What is compassion? It isn't pity for self or others. It isn't sympathy—having the same feelings for others. It isn't a version of empathy—understanding the feelings of another. Compassion is the inner expression of knowing what a person might be feeling and holding a place of love in support of that person's experience. By being compassionate, you are helping that person move from suffering to relief.

One of my favorite essays is *The Compassionate Instinct*, by Dacher Keltner. In it, Keltner says,

> *Compassion* is a powerful judgment-free motivator and a biological experience.
>
> *Compassion* slows our heart-beat down and we secrete oxytocin, the bonding hormone. This hormone is the nurturing hormone that makes us want to care for others.

Buddhists believe that you can't fully have compassion for others until you have compassion for yourself. Kristin Neff, a researcher and author of the book *Self-Compassion*, says,

> ...self-compassion is a powerful way to achieve emotional well-being and contentment in our lives, helping us avoid destructive patterns of fear, negativity, and isolation. More so than self-esteem, the nurturing quality of self-compassion allows us to flourish, to appreciate the beauty and richness of life, even in hard times. When we soothe our agitated minds with self-compassion, we're better able to notice what's right as well as what's wrong, so that we can orient ourselves toward that which gives us joy.

How about self-compassion? Do you know what that feels like?
Do you take a moment when you're beating up on yourself and
just sit in your heart in compassion?

Being Compassion

At times we may cross wires while having compassion and attach
another person's emotion to our own story. This isn't helpful to
anyone. If you are the person holding compassion, if you match
another person's suffering, then both of you are in suffering. To
be compassion is to hold open the loving space of acceptance for
that person to heal.

Compassion comes from the heart and the heart is open, free,
and non-judgmental. It feels expansive. Compassion is the ability
to hold an open space for another, to listen and to witness their
pain so they can release it, dissolve it, and allow it to be on its way
to love.

Compassion for others begins with compassion for self. We are
spiritual beings having a human experience. Love yourself with
grace and forgiveness for all you've done out of harmony with
the truth of what you really are—perfect.

Affirmation:

I am compassion embodied. I freely give compassion to myself. I freely give compassion to others.

Compassion is not a relationship between the healer and the wounded. It's a relationship between equals. Only when we know our own darkness well can we be present with the darkness of others. Compassion becomes real when we recognize our shared humanity.

—Pema Chodron

Deep breath.

24

Embrace Mistakes and Failures

Mistakes are unavoidable, and when viewed as positive they turn into valuable wisdom. Aren't they just learning opportunities?

Mistakes are subconsciously designed experiences to help us learn and evolve. Admitting your mistakes to others can be a powerful practice that frees yourself from judgment. Once a mistake is exposed and you take personal responsibility for it, you are free to learn and move on. If you admit your mistakes with others, they may choose to do the same, freeing everyone from the stressful emotions of guilt, shame, disappointment, and judgment.

> *Fall down seven times, stand up eight.*
>
> —Japanese Proverb

Think of a mistake you made recently. What emotions come up when you think about it? Are you judging yourself? Criticizing yourself?

Turn mistakes and failures into wisdom:

1. Sit down with a sheet of paper and write one mistake per page.

2. On each page write down your thoughts, beliefs, and emotions about that failure.

3. Practice self-forgiveness. How? By sitting with these feeling and emotions and being willing to let go. Do this repeatedly until there is no longer an emotional

charge. (See practice 30, for the Sacred Holding exercise.)

Forgiveness is the key to happiness.

—A Course in Miracles

Affirmation:
I forgive myself for my perception of a mistake and I turn it into valuable wisdom. I am forgiven now.

I've come to believe that all my past failures and frustrations were actually laying the foundation for the understandings that have created the new level of living I now enjoy.

—Anthony Robbins

25

Celebrate Your Value

The ego thinks there is a measurement of self-worth. The ego judges, compares, and criticizes in the context of our life experience and cultural norms. Up to now, your perceived value has likely been tainted by your ego. This perception is not who you are but rather who your ego thinks you are.

You may be tempted to gauge your value on the suffering you've experienced in your life, skills you've learned, accomplishments you've made, and battles you've won. You can radically simplify your life by basing your value on the love in your heart and your ability to be present for others.

Embracing and celebrating your unique talents and gifts allows you to acknowledge your own value. When you can see your own brilliance it's much easier to embrace your self-worth. Remember that there is no other person like you. You are the only person who can deliver the beautiful essence of *you* into the world.

It does take work to break the self-criticizing habits of a lifetime, but at the end of the day, you are only being asked to relax, allow life to be as it is, and open your heart to yourself. It's easier than you might think, and it could change your life.

—Kristin Neff

Your true value is based on feeling love in your heart for yourself and exercising your ability to share that love with others. It comes from within. How you see and value yourself is how you see and value others. Wouldn't it be nice to tune that up and live in your full power?

When you undervalue what you do, the world will undervalue who you are.

—Oprah Winfrey

Embrace Your Value

Once you know who you are and what you stand for, it's easier to feel like you have your own navigation system and are living in your own power. Everything you think, say, and do feels true in your heart. When you feel true, you are in alignment with your authentic self.

Live in Accordance to Your Value

Your value is an inner knowing and not something that is created or altered by the outer world.

There is *only one you*, with an inner calling to live this life in joy. Make it a habit to live in alignment with the wisdom in your heart. Stand firm in your inner knowing.

Affirmation:
I see my value; I am valued.

A diminished self-image causes us to slouch, to avoid looking others in the eye, to be unassertive, to be indecisive. On the other hand, a healthy self-image causes us to carry ourselves well, to speak confidently and to portray dignity. If we have not taken the time and thought to create a wonderful self-image for ourselves, we have had less, been less, and done less than was possible for us than if we had. We can improve our self-images at any moment including this one.

—Wu Wei

You're love.

26

Ask for What You Need

What is this thing inside many of us that causes us not to ask for what we need? Is it that we don't want to bother others or seem needy? Is it that we don't want to burden someone else with our problems?

Hmmmm. This behavior of not asking for what we need completely disrupts human relationships.

In order for us to be there for one another in a healthy way, we need to express what it is we need while giving the other person the freedom to state whether he or she can deliver on our request.

If you feel like you need a hug instead of a lecture, say so. People love delivering on what someone else really needs. Instead of making people guess, just tell them what you need and watch how easy it is to attract. For example, you could say,

- I need you to just listen.
- I need you to hold me.
- I need you to take care of this for me.
- I need you to dance with me.

Whatever the need, say it out loud and see what happens.

Affirmation:
I ask for what I want and need.

You will know who truly loves you when you ask them to do an unconventional favor.

—Michael Bassey Johnson

It's in the Letting Go

Sometimes letting things go is an act of far greater power than defending or hanging on.

—Eckhart Tolle

Letting Go Creates an Opening for New Energy, New Life

Imagine a trapeze artist who swings out to grab the incoming bar and, in a split second, decides not to let go of the bar she's hanging on to. The result? Either she dangles backward, or falls to the net. Neither gives her what she originally aimed for.

There is an art to letting go. First, you must have a compelling reason. Second, you must act. Being willing to let go and making the move to let go are profoundly different choices. Make the choice—hang on for dear life or propel yourself into the future.

Afterward you will likely say, "That wasn't so hard!"

Sit still.

27

Let Go of Outcomes

As you become intentional with your manifestations, you will likely have a defined picture of what you want. This doesn't necessarily mean that you will receive a direct match to your vision. The universe has a way of delivering things quite literally and a little askew.

The trick to manifesting is to let go of outcomes. By all means, have a clear vision of what you want, then let go of what transpires. The reason for this is that the universe may give you something even better than you imagined. If you hold stubborn expectations of having things a certain way, you may completely miss how the universe responds to you.

Letting go of outcomes is a practice that also brings you peace. It reduces and may even eliminate expectations, which always get you in trouble. If you lived your life free from expectations of others' actions or how the world should treat you, can you imagine the peace you would have inside? That is the gift and the power of letting go of outcomes.

Practice letting go of your expectations for one entire day and see how that improves your peace of mind. Let go. Just let go. The energy of anticipation is much more fun than the energy of expectation. Think about it.

Affirmation:
I am letting go of outcomes now. I receive what is given.

We must be willing to let go of
the life we have planned, so as to accept
the life that is waiting for us.

—Joseph Campbell

28

Let in Something New

Once you've let go, celebrate by giving yourself something new—maybe a bouquet of flowers, a new piece of art, a new tool or toy. Go ahead, do it.

Why? Because now that you've let go of something (emotionally or physically) that no longer serves you, you have room for what you really desire. This is a practice in how the universe works, in how you create space for the new to come in. Your action of letting go opens doors to fresh air, to more energy, and to possibility. Let it in.

Take your time and relish the experience of giving yourself something you long for. This is a gift that you're giving yourself. You are honoring yourself and giving yourself pleasure. It's a good thing!

Receiving is an act that balances life. If you're a giver, you must take time to receive in order to honor flow and the divine nature of the universe.

Affirmation:

I receive all things coming into my life that are in accordance with my highest and best interest.

When you clench your fist, no one can put anything in your hand, nor can your hand pick up anything.

—Alex Haley

29

Breathe to Re-Balance
(8-Breath ReBoot)

You can bring yourself into balance at any moment. The following breathing exercise is an amazing way to re-ground yourself quickly and easily. This method also brings you into the present and helps to calm you.

Do the following to perform the **8-Breath ReBoot**:

- Access some fresh air.

- Breathe in slowly, through the nose, for a count of eight.

- Hold the breath for eight counts.

- Make an "O" with your lips and bend forward as you slowly exhale through the mouth for eight counts— flushing impurities from your body. Push energy from the pit of your stomach. Lean forward and push out any remaining air.

- Return to an upright position. Hold no breath for eight counts.

- Repeat three times, or more if you feel you have a lot to release.

As you do this breath work, pay attention to the energy moving inside you. Allow any emotions that you no longer need to arise. Then release them.

Affirmation:
I am grounded, calm, and centered.

Feelings come and go like clouds in a windy sky.
Conscious breathing is my anchor.

—Thich Nhat Hanh

30

Forgive the Self
(Sacred Holding)

There are times in life when we can benefit from letting ourselves off the hook—through self-forgiveness and forgiveness for others. Forgiveness is the ability to sit in the heart with a specific pain or suffering or self-judgment, to witness it, and to watch it dissolve or lessen its grip. It's compassion for the self that opens the heart and releases strife.

FORGIVENESS. *Compassionate feelings that support a willingness to forgive.* [1]

Here is a gentle practice for forgiveness that was taught to me by a Sufi teacher.

For the practice of **Sacred Holding** do the following:

1. Close your eyes and take three slow, deep breaths, releasing what you no longer need.

2. Bring an instance of pain/suffering/judgment into your consciousness.

3. Feel it in the body. Tune in to where you feel this pain.

4. Now, sit with this pain, witness it. Hold your attention on the emotion. It will begin to release or dissolve.

---

[1] *Wordnet 3.0, Farlex clipart collection*, s.v. "forgiveness," accessed April 19, 2017, http://www.thefreedictionary.com/Forgiveness.

5. Once the emotion has released from your body, try to bring it up again. If there is still emotion, sit with it again until it releases. Do this until you can no longer bring it up.

Congratulations! You've started the process of self-healing and just healed yourself. Each time you feel one of these negative emotions, step into self-forgiveness and practice Sacred Holding. You will find that your pain/suffering/judgments turn from self-abuse to self-compassion, and from blame to love.

Affirmation:
I release myself from self-judgments. I release the need to blame. I am forgiveness. I am forgiven.

The weak can never forgive.
Forgiveness is the attitude of the strong.

—Mahatma Gandhi

Presence Changes Everything

The most precious gift we can offer others is our presence. When mindfulness embraces those we love, they will bloom like flowers.

—Thich Nhat Hanh

In a Busy World, Presence Is a Rare Experience

What is the value of presence? Without presence nothing is truly connected, and being in alignment can't happen. If we spend our time multi-tasking, over-doing, and running about without focus, we expend huge amounts of energy and can leave ourselves with little to give.

When Eckhart Tolle wrote *The Power of Now*, a western audience began to realize that there was indeed a practice of presence that would change everything. This awareness was the discovery that everything lives in the present moment.

Being in the present moment connects you with all that is.

Be here.

31

The Power of Presence

This moment is all we have. It's so easy to let the mind wander to future lands and memories of the past. The mind loves to think it knows everything and can see all; yet it knows nothing about the bliss of the present moment. In one single moment everything is created.

When we are focused in this moment and are conscious of our thoughts and feelings, we create the next moment and our next experience. When we breathe consciously and focus on the breath we bring ourselves into the present moment.

To the mind it can feel as though we're avoiding getting things done. The time can feel unproductive, meaningless, and slow. Yet everything we create stems from every thought and every feeling we have within each moment.

This space where we can just *be* is called peace. It is said that we can only find true happiness inside of this moment, then inside of the next, and the next, and so on. There has been plenty written about being in the present moment, but how much of this wisdom do you practice in your day?

Be Present

Practice presence. Stop. Take a breath. Close your eyes. Focus on your body in this moment. Just feel. Breathe in the air that supports you. Exhale the busyness of your mind. Stay here for a bit, creating this moment, then the next.

Do you feel at peace? Practice presence and see how it changes the outcomes of your interactions. Let your mind rest. Just *be* while you're doing. I know you can do it.

Affirmation:
I am in the present moment.

You must live in the present, launch yourself on every wave, find your eternity in each moment.

—Henry David Thoreau

32

The Art of Non-Action

In our busy world, with many perceived tasks and responsibilities, we can literally kill ourselves with to-do lists. We can become ineffective at making decisions. We can be ungrounded and flirt with burnout. We can be the type of personality that loves lists—making them, adding things to them, crossing tasks off to feel a sense of accomplishment. Worse, we can thrive on the emotion of struggle.

Our culture is about achievement. This is the way of pushing, versus flowing with the natural order of things. Wu Wei, a Taoist philosophy, teaches that through non-doing and stillness one can be in alignment with the natural energy and flow of life.

If you live your life in harmony with the seasons you will live naturally and not force things; you will be in the world in a natural rhythm; you will pace yourself, pause, reflect, and allow space for new information to come in and for old to be released. What would that be like for you?

Practice not-doing and everything will fall into place.

Get out of the way and do nothing. Sit in stillness. Here's how:

1. Disengage with the world.

2. Sit still.

3. Nurture yourself into the quiet.

4. Listen, deeply listen to what your higher self (not your busy mind) has to share with you.

5. When you come out of this experience, give. Give of your wisdom.

If you are a business person, learn to delegate, be patient and wait for things to unfold naturally. As you practice this new way of being you will finally arrive at non-action.

Affirmation:
I trust the stillness. I trust the natural flow of life.

The more exquisitely and delightfully you can do nothing, the higher your life's achievement.

—Elizabeth Gilbert

33

Open Your Mind

The ego mind loves to put parameters around things, to define things, label things, and to create its identity based on things, thereby boxing you in. When you let go of the needs of the ego you are left with an openness, an expansiveness, and a sense of wonder.

Maintaining a state of openness can relieve judgment and free you up to receive. Imagine a box around your head that contains all of your shoulds and have-tos. Then imagine an open field extending out from the front and back of your heart. Which would you prefer to live in—the box or the field?

Take ten minutes to try this exercise:

Open to the field of dreams.... Sit in an open field and see the beauty in nature—the grass, flowers, trees. Feel the sunshine and the warm air. Listen to the sounds in your field. What comes to you?

Affirmation:
I am open and receiving what the universe has to show me.

Let yourself be open and life will be easier. A spoon of salt in a glass of water makes the water undrinkable. A spoon of salt in a lake is almost unnoticed.

—Buddha Siddhartha Guatama Shakyamuni

34

Strive for Balance

A constant ebb and flow of energy—thoughts, emotions, actions—these things create movement in your life. They dance in and out, up and down, and sideways. It can seem nearly impossible at times to find balance in this chaotic world, but the truth is that balance is within you.

It may be helpful to know a little about how the Chinese have viewed energy for thousands of years. The yin and yang philosophy states that the energy in the universe is made up of two opposing yet complementary forces. These forces are in a constant and fluid state of flux with each other, creating a whole. One cannot exist without the other. For examples consider dark and light, feminine and masculine, sun and moon, earth and cosmos.

If you consider what balance means within the interplay between these energies, you realize that to find balance you must begin with thoughts, feelings, and emotions. What you think can cause you to tip one way or the other—to the positive or negative side of an experience. To achieve balance, you must find the middle ground.

Practicing Buddhists call this the Middle Way, also known as a practice of moderation, which is said to eliminate suffering. It is the way of non-attachment, letting go of the outcomes, maintaining neutrality in the face of conflict, and not going overboard with excitement. Think of it like a pendulum. If it swings far in one direction, by natural law it must swing the same distance in the other direction. To maintain a steady, mild swing, the energy that is within it has to calm down and be increasingly still.

How can you create this kind of balance in your life? What does it feel like to find your center and stay there most of the time?

Find Your Center

When things in life trigger you or tip you over, try this:

- Take a deep breath.

- Become an observer.

- Keep breathing slowly—in and out.

- Imagine yourself sitting in your heart, in your chest.

- Connect to your center. Feel more peace.

- If you're in the presence of another person, observe, listen, and ask questions that help that person feel seen, heard, and loved. Doing this for another will bring a sense of peace to you.

Affirmation:
I am in balance at all times. I live the Middle Way.

To find the balance you want, this is what you must become. You must keep your feet grounded so firmly on the earth that it's like you have 4 legs instead of 2. That way, you can stay in the world. But you must stop looking at the world through your head. You must look through your heart, instead. That way, you will know God.

—Elizabeth Gilbert

The Illuminated Life

Act as a model for life in accordance with your
highest light and more light will be given.

—Dan Millman

The word *illumine* is such a beautiful word. It invites you think of a brilliant golden flame, light, and all things made of love. To live an illuminated life means to strive for higher thought, kindness, compassion, service to others, and making the world a better place. It requires a commitment to heal your wounds and leave victimhood behind.

An illuminated life is one where you have consciously evolved and consistently chosen to be your absolute best. It does not mean being perfect. It means being conscious, awake, and committed to practicing higher thought, and living in accordance with universal laws.

As a divine spark of God, you already are illuminated—it's a matter of how you choose to shine in the world. We each have free will to experience this earth life in any way we wish. If you're reading this book, it's highly likely that you already ascribe to many of the ideas within these pages. The question is, how are you doing with your practice? Could you use a more dedicated plan to live an illuminated life?

Light.

35

Inner Illumination

We feel most alive when we feel illuminated, light. When we are illuminated we are open to receive, we are breathing, we are in our hearts, we have no expectations, we are grateful, we are at peace.

Illumination occurs when we connect to the natural energy that flows in the body. It's always there to access and build upon.

Using the Power of the Heart to Light Up the World

According to the Institute of HeartMath, the heart is the largest oscillating organ in the body. It has enough power to light a lightbulb and to draw things to it. Imagine a room of grandfather clocks. The largest and most powerful clock has the power to entrain all the other clocks to its rhythm. Your heart has the same ability. When you are illuminated from your heart you can draw everything around you into your rhythm.

When you're not in your heart (and you're in your head) you have less power and less illumination. It takes more energy to live and operate from the head (mind/ego).

You get to choose. Do you want to live in illumination and realize greater results? Or do you want to dim your world to mediocre?

Affirmation:
I am in my heart—feeling its power and allowing it to draw good things to me.

Seek for illumination of self, and then the world, through the simple, humble, almighty, supreme virtue of love.

—Bryant McGill

36

The Power of Optimism

Let's explore optimism. As you likely know, positivity begets positivity. If you want more, then find more. Begin by looking within yourself. If you can't find positivity within yourself, surround yourself with others who have it until they influence you with their inner glow.

Positivity Is Attractive

We love to be around people who are positive. When you're negative, positive people either shy away from you or try to get you to be more positive. If you look at positivity (a higher vibration) as an energy force, you will see that what does not match its vibration will move on to find its own vibrational match. It's the law of the universe.

A higher vibration is a higher vibration! If you haven't already, make sure to read practice 11, *Raising Your Vibration*, as it will turn a bad day into a great day! It's within your power to do so. Even when you're feeling blue you can shift to a little higher vibration by seeing things differently. Your emotions will then shift and your outcomes will be of a higher frequency. Wow! Yes, you do have that kind of magic at your fingertips!

Where do you want to vibrate? What type of experience do you want?

Affirmation:
I am positive and hold my optimistic force field no matter what.

There are two ways of spreading light: to be the candle or the mirror that reflects it.

—Edith Wharton

37

Joy Creates More Joy

It's a simple idea: joy creates more joy. If you believe that the universe is a construct of vibration, then happiness, laughter, and joy are high vibrations, and distress, anger, guilt, and shame are low vibrations. Under the principle of *like attracts like*, truly being in the high vibration of joy will create more joy.

Here's the catch. You can't fake it! If you're not feeling joy within your heart and throughout your body, you cannot create more joy.

Do this exercise to create more joy:

1. Ask yourself, "What experience have I had in my life that was filled with joy?"

2. Close your eyes and take three deep breaths. Breathe in joy. Breathe out what isn't joy.

3. Now, sit and recall this time of joy and feel it in your body. Feel it until your heart sings.

4. Hold this vibration for as long as possible.

Throughout your day focus on the following affirmation and remember your fond memory of joy. Stay in the moment and you will lift your spirit and be in joy. Being in joy is a choice.

Affirmation:
I am in joy right now.

Joy is the holy fire that keeps our purpose warm
and our intelligence aglow.

—Helen Keller

38

Expect Magic

Expecting magic implies living in a state of wonderment and curiosity with an open mind. When you practice being in the moment, joy infiltrates your experience. If you lighten up on your *adulting*, you can find yourself in a playful, silly mood. Joy invites magic and magic is the mindset of living in the world of constant learning.

Typically, children younger than seven are not limited by social norms and expectations. They are free to be whatever they choose to be. After seven, the world begins to shape your behavior. As an adult, it's up to you to unwind this conditioning and allow yourself to play, wonder, experiment, and create. Joy leads to bliss. More joy brings more bliss.

Today is your day to expect magic and to watch what happens! Here are a few tips for being open to magic:

- Get in your heart by focusing on something you love.

- Think of things that bring you joy.

- Get into a state of childlike wonder with play.

- Act like you're on a scavenger hunt.

- Watch with curious anticipation during your interactions with others.

- Create something—anything.

- Play with a child.

- Skip down the street.
- Dance to your favorite song.

Get your wonderment on and have a great day!

Affirmation:
I am open to magic all day long.

I have always been delighted at the prospect of a new day, a fresh try, one more start, with perhaps a bit of magic waiting somewhere behind the morning.

—J. B. Priestley

Master What It Takes

Whenever you want to achieve something, keep your eyes open, concentrate and make sure you know exactly what it is you want. No one can hit their target with their eyes closed.

—Paulo Coelho

Your conscious brain is faced with choices every nanosecond of every day. There are some disciplines that will make your way of being in the world a little easier, but that doesn't mean these disciplines are easy.

When it comes to aspirations like focus, consistency, discipline, and decisiveness, the demand is that we shift from unconscious patterns to conscious habits. To change an unhealthy behavior, we have to build the muscle of discipline.

You can do this!

Choose.

39

Decisiveness

Decisiveness means diving into a choice with your whole self—mind, body, and soul. When you are decisive you are committed. Just writing those words feels serious!

What is it in our human nature that makes us squirm at the thought of commitment? Do we think we will lose something? Lose control? Lose out? Lose joy?

What is it in our human nature that makes us indecisive? Fear of making a mistake? A fear of being unloved? Fear of it not being the right decision? Indecision causes confusion for all.

Once you decide, everything and everyone around you will become clear. A decision serves as a stake in the ground that tells the universe, "This is what I intend." The universe then goes to work on making that happen and creating a manifestation. Deciding gets you a result. It makes things happen. Are you willing to decide and accept the outcome?

Let's look more closely at the definitions for these words.

DECIDE. *To make a judgment or determine a preference; come to a conclusion.* [2]
COMMIT. *To pledge (oneself) to a position on an issue or question; express (one's intention, feeling, etc).* [3]

What is one decision in your life right now that would change

---

[2] *Dictionary.com*, s.v. "decide, def. 5," accessed April 4, 2017,
http://www.dictionary.com/browse/decide?s=t.

[3] *Dictionary.com*, "commit, def. 3," accessed April 4, 2017,
http://www.dictionary.com/browse/commit?s=t.

everything for the better? If you're courageous enough, put this book down right now and do it. Take action.

What is the one thing in your life right now that you could commit to that would shift an unconscious habit into a conscious choice? What is it? How long do you want to commit to it? What does commitment look like if it were 100%? Are you ready? Do it now. Make a commitment and begin to act.

Affirmation:
I am committed to my chosen path. I decide with fierce determination.

To be decisive means to do it with every part of your being, or don't do it at all.

—Dr. J.D. Stone and Rev. Gloria Excelcias

40

Focus

The practice of focus brings us into the present moment and allows us to follow through on an intent. When we are not focused, we can become scattered, overwhelmed, and ineffective.

When you realize you're not focused, take a deep, cleansing breath and come fully into this moment in the body. Feel your body where you're sitting, standing, or lying. Become present with yourself. Then do one thing at a time and follow through.

It helps to have little reminders strung about when you're working on focus—maybe post-it notes stuck to your walls, mirrors, doors, and computer.

Notice how you feel when you focus and follow through. Do you feel more grounded? Do you feel more successful? Do you feel like you can get something done?

Most people have no idea of the giant capacity we
can immediately command when we focus
all of our resources on mastering
a single area of our lives.

—Anthony Robbins

41

Consistency

What is consistency? How do you define it? Once you understand your own definition of consistency you can see if you have some refining to do.

Consider using this concise definition:

CONSISTENCY. *Reliability or uniformity of successive results or event.* [4]

How consistent are you?

- When you look at how you're manifesting, assess how reliable you are at taking action steps.

- How regular are you in your approach?

- Do you have a daily practice that is consistent, one that allows your mind and the universe to count on you?

To ensure consistency, evaluate your daily practice and see if you need to tune it up. The value of consistency is that it is core to the success of your intentional manifestations. The practice of consistency also shows your ego mind that you are serious about your goals, that you are constant in your pursuit of what you truly want.

---

[4] *Thefreedictionary.com,* "consistency, def. 2," accessed April 4, 2017, http://www.thefreedictionary.com/consistency.

Affirmation:
I am committed to my consistency to create the results I desire.

Perfection of effort is not required, by the way. It is the consistency of attempting to work these tools that brings the progress. It's like anything else. If I want to tone muscle, lifting a ten-pound weight a few times every day will move me toward my goal much quicker than hoisting a fifty-pound barbell once a week. Yes, it really is true: "Slow and steady wins the race." Just try a little, every day. You'll see.

—Holly Mosier

42

Discipline

Let's just let go of the idea that being disciplined is a pain in the behind. Just let it go. Once you let it go you can address the business at hand.

Discipline is the cornerstone of making your dreams come true. I personally like a spontaneous life, but that doesn't equate to getting things done and making *it* happen. Discipline does not have to be a masculine, forceful endeavor. It can be a gentle practice of consistent action that reaps results.

To create discipline for your dream, establish a regular time every day at which you focus on your vision for your life. This could be for three minutes in the morning. Then add one action step toward your dream each day. Make the step doable. This focus and small step can lead to the unveiling of your dream right before your eyes. Why? Because the universe is listening. The universe responds to your consistent focus and attention.

Be disciplined in your actions toward your dream and you will see your dream come to fruition. To test your progress ask yourself each day, "What have I accomplished in the forward movement of my dream?" and "What's different today?"

Affirmation:
I am disciplined, intentional, and focused.

We are what we repeatedly do,
excellence then is not an act, but a habit.

—Aristotle

43

Pace

Everything I've learned about pacing myself has been affirmed by a herd of 130 elk that frequent my front door. As I observe their true nature, I witness their times to eat, to rest, to play, mate, and to roam.

There is a rhythm that they abide by and no one or thing stands in their way of this natural state of being. They are not in a hurry. They are in the present moment, taking care of the desire at hand. They stay together, watch out for one another, and carry on about their day.

They follow the path of abundant nourishment. They are rarely ever alone.

- What would you do differently if you were pacing yourself in a way that matched your natural rhythms?

- Who would you include in your tribe?

- Who watches out for you?

- How do you nourish yourself?

Your task is to pick one of the above questions and contemplate your answer. If you are inspired to do so, choose one thing that you will do to begin to pace yourself better. Maybe you can take a little extra time for lunch or make time to visit with a friend or co-worker. You decide.

You will feel more balanced and less stressed once you see that you can pace yourself. You are in charge of your pace.

Affirmation:
I pace myself in a way that serves my personal energy needs.

Rivers know this: there is no hurry.
We shall get there someday.

—Winnie-the-Pooh

44

Patience

Taking your dreams from the world of ideas into the world of physical manifestation takes constant focus and continued faith. You need patience as you bridge your excited anticipation of your dreams coming true and the reality of creating them. As you take steps to move your dreams forward, there are times you will need to wait to receive results. During this time it is key to have patience, and to fill the space of patience with a positive emotion.

Everything that manifests does so by energy, by emotion, and by igniting the *like attracts like* manifestation law. If you're trying to be patient but find it challenging, focus on Holding the Field— hold the energy, the intent, and the desired outcome strong while you practice patience.

Previously we talked about letting go of the outcome. You can let go of the outcome and still hold the field strong with your intent.

Affirmation:

I am patient. I gracefully accept the pace at which my dreams unfold.

Patience is not the ability to wait.
Waiting is a fact of life.
Patience is the ability to keep a
good attitude while waiting.

—Joyce Meyers

Inner-Power Tools

The courage to do it anyway,
lifts your wings and sets your flight.

—Anonymous

As we grow in this life, we learn. We make mistakes, and we learn some more. Wisdom comes when we decide to integrate what we've learned deep in our soul. Along the way there is spiritual muscle building. Tenacity, courage, integrity, and other inner-power tools are gifts we gain as we learn to live fully in our own personal power. They come to us with practice.

Dedication, consistency, and commitment to our own growth reaps great rewards. We earn our stripes as we stay the course. As we gain strength, we simply begin to soar in the divine light of who we authentically are.

Be whole.

45

Integrity
(Wholeness)

Integrity is one of the most vital topics of this book—not only because integrity is a significant value, but because it may cause you to ponder a notion you haven't really thought about.

The act of being in integrity requires great personal responsibility. Integrity means wholeness—the state of being whole or undiminished. To support things as whole, you must strive to keep things whole. To be whole is to be in joy, to be happy.

If you reprimand someone because you think they did something wrong, you've just destroyed wholeness. If you judge someone because you don't agree with the way they do things, you've chipped away at wholeness. If you think a negative thought about someone, you violate that person's integrity, their wholeness, and damage your own wholeness and joy in the process.

You lose integrity when you pick things apart, criticize, judge, blame, make-wrong, and assign negative emotion to a person or a situation. The more you do this, the less whole everything around you becomes. In other words, when there is a breach of integrity things tend to fall apart and go out of alignment. If integrity is greatly lacking, then great distress with a person or situation will ensue.

Here are some tips to stay in integrity:

• When you get triggered, try to return to neutral as quickly as possible. Check in with your body sensations and locate where you feel the distress. Once you locate this place in the body, breathe into it, slowly, in and out a few times until you feel the sensation release.

- When you have a negative thought about someone, stop and replace it with gratitude, joy, laughter, and love.

- When you feel judged or criticized, go into an observation mode, as if the event is happening but it's happening outside of you and you're not affected by it. Try being in your own bubble.

This isn't about being superhuman. It's about increasing your level of consciousness and shifting your behavior toward bliss (more on that coming up).

Another way of looking at integrity is doing what you say you are going to do. When you make a small intentional statement, like "I'm going to call my mother now," and then you don't do it, maybe you don't call her until the following day, you've just broken your integrity (wholeness). When this happens, the result is less joy, maybe even a nagging feeling that hangs with you until you call her.

This is a subtle look into integrity, yet you can see how breaking wholeness can happen in a number of ways in our daily lives. How much do you want to be in integrity? Is it one of your top values? If so, how do you describe it?

Affirmation:
I am in integrity at all times with my thoughts,
words, and actions.

The law of integrity is about living in line with
your highest vision despite impulses to the
contrary—about how you behave
when no one is watching.

—Dan Millman

Be strong.

46

Tenacity

There are times in your life when you must reach deep down and pull up every resource you have to take the next step. These times require sheer tenacity. There is a saying that God will never give you more than you can handle. Do you feel that you can handle all that is before you? If you answered yes, congratulate yourself for being one of the brave and courageous souls that moves through resistance no matter what.

Tenacity doesn't have to mean that you ignore the signs that clearly tell you to stop what you are doing. Tenacity means that when things get tough you move through the situation with awareness and lack of fear.

Where is your tolerance for tenacity? What makes you push through no matter what? When you know your own level of tenacity, you can choose what things are important to push through and what things you're better off letting go.

Affirmation:
I am tenacious. I am wise.

Let me tell you the secret that has led me to my goal. My strength lies solely in my tenacity.

—Louis Pasteur

47

Perseverance

PERSEVERANCE. *Steady persistence in adhering to a course of action, a belief, or a purpose; steadfastness.* [5]

Perseverance is key to unfolding and manifesting your dreams. With consistent focus and action steps that are aligned to your goals, you ignite the law of attraction, which brings to you your intention. In other words, being persistent is an energetic action that funnels an intent into an emotional and physical action, which causes the effect of a result.

If you are working on a goal, a task, or a step of a larger project when you apply perseverance, you can't help but get results. What results are you currently getting? When you look at the results in your life you can see what you're manifesting, and what you're manifesting is a direct result of your intentions.

To maintain the kind of perseverance that reaps the results you want, focus on what you want in direct relation to your desires.

---

[5] *Thefreedictionary.com*, "perseverance, def. 1," accessed April 4, 2017, http://www.thefreedictionary.com/consistency.

Affirmation:
I am persevering for my highest good.

I do not think there is any other quality so essential to success of any kind as the quality of perseverance. It overcomes almost everything, even nature.

—John D. Rockefeller

48

Gumption

I have a friend whose name is Steve. He talks about gumption and how to have more of it. In fact, my friend embodies the character Forrest Gump. Forrest, in the movie *Forrest Gump*, does things without thought. He just says, "Okay," then does that thing.

There is true power in not letting your ego mind seize your actions. Have you ever had the experience where you acted without listening to the mental banter? Where you leaped without doubt or fear and just did it? Where afterward you said, "Wow! that was easy?"

The ego mind loves to mess with us. So, when you keep the mind's thoughts at bay and just act, you have gumption! You go ahead and do it, and that action reaps results. Yay! Try it again and again and again and see what starts to unfold in your life.

Gumption can be viewed as guts, courage, moxie. When it comes down to it, gumption is stepping forward with faith and lack of concern for what might happen. Gumption—gotta love it!

Affirmation:
I have gumption. I act free of fear.

There are only 3 things that can make your dreams come true: your thoughts, your words, and your actions.

—Mike Dooley

49

Courage

How does one get courage? How does one show courage in the face of adversity? How does one muster courage to tackle the small tasks that seem too large to face?

Courage is a form of faith that carries energy capable of dismissing the illusion of entrapment. Courage is the type of energy that faces the storm, much like the way in which a bison faces into the winter snows. To enable the energy of courage we must dismiss impossibility. Courage is focused, determined, and unapologetic. Courage creates freedom.

Identify Courage

Identify who's the most courageous person in your world. Maybe it's someone you know. Maybe it's you. Take a moment to think about this person and tune into the energy of courage.

- How does it make you feel? Bigger than life? Invincible? Determined?

- How can you use this energy of courage to power your next move in life or business?

- How will you know when you've done it? How will you know what result it created for you?

Do this exercise to turn up your courage. Watch what happens.

Affirmation:
I am courageous.

With courage, you will dare to take risks, have the strength to be compassionate, and the wisdom to be humble. Courage is the foundation of integrity.

—Mark Twain

Skills of the Master

When you reach the end of your rope,
tie a knot and hang on.

—Abraham Lincoln

Never let them see you sweat. The spiritual warrior at some point decides to consistently use the skills she has learned. This choice often comes from hard-earned life experiences that have opened her up, sometimes through life events that seem nearly unbearable. Using the tools, practicing the skills, honing the knowledge, and turning lessons into wisdom is the stuff that masters are made of.

Elevate.

50

Stop Leaning—Start Standing

It is human nature to lean forward, to push, to reach out, and to be in the future instead of the present. When we do this we throw ourselves off balance—we lose our center. Leaning forward also symbolizes that we are not enough.

If you physically stop and stand up straight, you will feel your entire life force come into stillness. Your brain will think new things. You will be able to focus on what *IS* instead of thinking about what will be. You become more sovereign in your energy.

When you are not sovereign you lean on others for support. When you lean on them too much you begin to unconsciously drain their life force, and they can eventually become depleted. It's not their job to hold you up.

It's important to stand in your own energy field, to be responsible and conscious with your perceived needs. Victimhood and self-pity are two powerful energy drainers. They can suck the life out of relationships. If you take up permanent residence in these emotions, those around you will eventually begin to move away. No one can fill your tank for you. You have to do that for yourself.

It's nice to know there are people in your life that will love and support you, but don't kill them! You can always get a loving lift from others, but then take responsibility and stand tall. Your strength and determination shows others they can do the same.

Your mission is to get into alignment with your God self, your inner power. You already are *all that*—a divine spark. Stand up right now. Open your heart and claim your Divinity. Let your faith in abundance fill your tank and know that within you is the God Source that is all you need. *Ever.*

Be strong enough to stand alone, be yourself enough to stand apart, but be wise enough to stand together when the time comes.

—Mark Amend

51

Grace under Fire

It's easy to find grace when things are going smoothly. It's when S*#T hits the fan that you need grace most. Accessing grace when in the heat of an experience requires a master to come forth. What tricks might we explore that will help you move from garbage brain to grace?

Grace is a state of being. To access grace you first need to stop and drop into yourself. Breathe and be in the moment. Then wiggle your way from your head to your heart. Think of something peaceful and filled with grace. Maybe you think of God, the birds flying outside your window, or the wind blowing in the trees.

Grace is everywhere if you take the time to look. The funny thing is, when you bring yourself to the present moment you realize there is nothing to do but just be.

Life tosses you what you put out, so find a bit more grace and see what comes your way.

Affirmation:
I am in a state of grace.

To offer no resistance to life is to be in a state of grace, ease, and lightness. This state is then no longer dependent upon things being in a certain way, good or bad. It seems almost paradoxical, yet when your inner dependency on form is gone, the general conditions of your life, the outer forms, tend to improve greatly. Things, people, or conditions that you thought you needed for your happiness now come to you with no struggle or effort on your part, and you are free to enjoy and appreciate them—while they last. All those things, of course, will still pass away, cycles will come and go, but with dependency gone there is no fear of loss anymore. Life flows with ease.

—Eckhart Tolle

52

Yield

One of the most powerful skills a master can use is learning to yield. Yes, step back, pause, hold that thought, zip those lips.

When is it a good idea to yield? Can you think of three situations where it would have benefited you to delay or reserve your thoughts, words, or actions?

To yield is an undervalued behavior that may just bring you everything you want. *Huh?* Think about it. When you yield you stop, step back, wait, and open up to what's next. When you don't yield, you move forward, push through, and ignore anything that might block you from progressing.

Yielding opens a space for what's naturally yours. If you yield with grace you create an opening to possibilities. If you yield with curiosity, you expect the unknown. If you yield with wisdom, you know that what is coming is a wonderful surprise and potentially a life-changing experience.

Yes, yielding is a powerful tool used to expand your reality, receive your bounty, and let the universe step in and show you how it's done.

Affirmation:
I am yielding to all and letting the universe step in.

True wisdom is marked by willingness to listen
and a sense of knowing when to yield.

—Elizabeth George

53

Go Neutral

If you find yourself in a situation that is unpleasant, stop and ask yourself, "Is my negative reaction to this situation really a battle I want to fight, or would I rather let it go?"

Many times in life you find yourself in situations where you can choose to react or to let it go. Here's the secret: whatever you focus on, you give energy to; and what you give energy to expands. If you find yourself in a negative situation, such as another person's drama or drama into which they are trying to pull you, you have a choice to join the game or to go neutral. Going neutral means that you do not engage, that you meet the situation from a place of neutrality while also holding a space of compassion for yourself and others. In this case there is no energy exchange.

When people come to you because they know they can engage you and drain your energy (energy vampires), they'll keep coming back. When you stop doing this and go neutral they stop drawing you in. It's no longer fun for them.

Now if it's you doing the drama drain on others, stop yourself, take a breath, get in your heart, and go to neutral. If you sit yourself down you will realize that the situation is a mirror. Go neutral and glean what you need to know about your own thinking that created such an experience in your world. What comes up for you?

Compassion is holding a place in your heart open for others to have their own experience, and for you to release your own triggers. Compassion is neutral.

Affirmation:
I am neutral. I am at peace.

Sometimes it's better to react with no reaction.

—Kushandwisdom

54

Listen

This topic is dedicated to the greatest listener I know, Michael Toms, of New Dimensions Radio. *I'm sure his spirit is touching this page right now, celebrating his contribution to the world with his magical skills of deep listening. Thank you, Michael, for all that you have given the world.*

Michael Toms spent decades interviewing the great spiritual minds of our time on his radio show. He interviewed over three thousand thought leaders, including the Dalai Lama, Joseph Campbell, Jane Goodall, Jean Houston, Maya Angelou, R. Buckminster Fuller, President Jimmy Carter, J. Krishnamurti, Alice Walker, Dr. Andrew Weil, Huston Smith, Matthew Fox, and so many more.

It was during some special moments sitting with Michael and his wife, Justine, in their home in California that I experienced the magic of what he called Deep Listening/Deep Questioning. He created a space of inquisitiveness with a twinkle in his eyes, as if he were hearing about the world for the first time. I knew in this time and space that I could say anything I wanted and there would be no judgment, no rebuttal, no argument, just listening. It opened my eyes to the power and joy of listening.

Michael believed that every person just wants to be seen, heard, and loved for who they are. He was a master at creating this experience. He was an expert at asking questions to pull the deeper truth from people's stories.

Michael believed that we can begin deep listening right now. He recommended to just take a couple of minutes, breathe deeply, slow yourself down, and listen—to yourself, to others, to nature. When this space is mindfully created, the deeper truth emerges.

When you don't blame people, you can see yourself in the other person. That helps us connect more completely.

—Michael Toms

One of the most valuable skills we can learn is how to listen with an open mind—from our heart and with the spaciousness evident in deep compassion.

When we create an energetic field of quiet anticipation, we open the door for others to speak authentically while feeling safe. Listening is one of the greatest gifts we can give each other.

Here's how it works:

- Ask, "What would you like to share with me today?" "What is on your mind?"
- Listen. Listen deeply.
- Reflect back, "What I heard you say...."
- Ask, "Is that what you wanted me to hear?"

When you do this you will experience this spaciousness in the conversation, and opening of the heart. This space is sacred and loving. Once you do it, you will never want to go back to talking, talking, talking, ever again.

Affirmation:
I listen with full attention, an open heart, and non-judgment.

A person who speaks as if he knows everything soon drives away his listeners. The Universe communicates itself to us in many ways, and sometimes, it is through the words of others. If we act the know-it-all, others may refrain from talking to us, and we may fail to get the message they could have given us.

—Wu Wei

Be willing.

55

Trust

At what point in a relationship, a project, an assignment, or a process do you begin to trust? What is your pattern of trust or distrust?

- Do you have a pattern of blind trust—trusting without thinking?

- Do you have a habit of distrust, i.e., a lack of trust in everything?

- Do you have a propensity to trust only after gathering a lot of data, or, simply, is your trust riddled with skepticism?

- Do you trust only when someone else seems to trust you first?

- Do you instill trust in others?

- What needs to happen for you to trust more?

Trust lives in your emotional body. It is constructed from your life experiences. The sum of your experiences defines your *trust factor*. This fact is worth evaluating as there is likely room in our lives to trust more—in ourselves and in others. We trust by learning; there will always be adjustments.

When you trust, you open the doors to positive occurrences. When you distrust, you close doors and attract distrust. To open doors of trust you need to heal your fears. A great question to ask yourself when you distrust is, "What's the worst that can happen if I trust?" The answer will give you the information you need to face your fears. Once you know the nature of your fears, you can bring awareness to them by talking with the person or people who may be involved.

Exposing your fears reduces their power. Trust is built when you have confidence in yourself, in others, and in your ability to stay true and keep your word. And, to tell the truth, lies beget more lies. When you doubt, you get a reflection of doubt and there is no longer trust. Bring your lack of trust into the open. Talk about it and ask another person to validate or invalidate your reasons for lacking trust. Then trust.

Trust yourself first. Trust your own discernment, but trust; otherwise, you will attract distrust and doubt.

Affirmation:
I trust myself and my own discernment.

The best way to find out if you can trust somebody is to trust them.

—Ernest Hemingway

Retrain the Brain

Thoughts are boomerangs, returning with precision to their source. Choose wisely which ones you throw.

—Unknown

By now, you have read many topics in this book and are practicing new ways of being. Congratulations! Consciousness is hard work, until you realize it isn't.

I say that *tongue in cheek* because the greatest spiritual practices are incredibly simple. It takes conscious effort to break free from conditioning, cultural norms, habits, and familiar ways of being. It takes commitment and discipline.

As conscious humans we are always dealing with the ego, and the ego, though based on our unique experience, has a mind of its own. It can sometimes feel like another person living inside our being. Once we arrive at a certain point in our conscious evolution, the ego finds its perfect role and our heart takes charge. Getting to this place is a very personal journey—as no two of us are the same, even though in the bigger scheme of things the journey back to truth is all the same.

I wondered, "Why have I been chasing happiness my whole life when bliss was here the entire time?"

—Elizabeth Gilbert

Be awake.

56

Conscious Words

Every word is a vibration. Every word shapes the energy field in the universe. If one word or many words are expressed with intense emotion, they can have exponential impact on shaping the energy field.

In the beginning was the Word,
and the Word was with God, and the Word was God.
(John 1:1)

Becoming conscious with the words you use is one of the most powerful practices you have for creating and contributing to a higher vibration universe in the likeness of God. As you speak a word consciously, you can sense its impact on others. Even if you think you can't, you can.

If you are aware and practicing your consciousness, on many levels you are feeling the vibrational frequency of the energy field around you. How intentional are you with your words? How clear are you with the words you want to use?

According to Robert Tennyson Stevens, in his book *Conscious Language: The Logos of Now*, words tend to be a left-brain function and feelings are a right-brain function. When we use words that are in balance between the left brain and the right brain (whole brain), we manifest that matching reality. If we consciously choose our words and feelings, we consciously co-create our reality for a higher purpose. If we are unconscious with our words and reckless with our feelings, we manifest that too.

"I" is God; "AM" is action.
"I" is right-brain; "AM" is left-brain.
"I AM" is whole brain.

—Robert Tennyson Stevens

Whenever you state "I AM" you are clearly stating your intent. If you use I AM without thought, you go out of alignment with higher thought and create a lower vibrational frequency. If you use I AM with great care and thought, you go into alignment with higher thought and create a life reflective of your authentic, divine self.

Affirmation:
I AM conscious with every word.

I AM,
two of the most powerful words; for whatever you
put after them shapes your reality.

—Unknown

57

Not That Thought

The mind is powerful. It can sometimes take you places you don't want to go. It can make up stories, justify things, and convince you of things that aren't true. It can also run wild.

So how do you tame the mind and bring it into a state of balance, peace, and calm? How do you bring it into alignment with the deep inner truth that you are already peace, you are already whole?

Stop. Drop. Roll.

Yes, that's what I said. There are times when you have to stop your mind from running wild by doing something to break your state. Tony Robbins calls this a pattern interrupt, as it is also known in the practice of Neuro-Linguistic Programming (NLP). This technique is designed to break the neural link between thought, emotion, and pattern.

To do this you need to create a physical action that gets your attention. I have worn a rubber band on my wrist that I could snap when I noticed my mind going into a habitual pattern. I have used music and dance to change my state. I have used nature, the breath, and walking to shift energy.

Your task is to select your own way of changing your state. Practice using your chosen technique to break your state for the next few days. You'll find that you will end up breaking a thought pattern, end up laughing, and maybe even releasing yourself from an old pattern.

Affirmation:
I am breaking my negative state now.

As soon as you have made a thought, laugh at it.

—Lao Tzu

58

Lifting Doubt

There are times when doubt creeps into our day. It's that niggly thought pattern that causes our faith to wobble. Doubt is the mind's way of keeping busy and causing havoc. Doubt is the language of the ego; it's fear. Is it real or imagined?

What shall we do when doubt seeps into our reality?

Dealing with doubt first requires your acknowledgment that it is present. Shining light on it begins to dissipate it. Once you recognize it, ask yourself what it would feel like if it wasn't present in that moment. Allow the gripping feeling doubt creates in your body to relax and release. Breathe into it. As this energy releases, affirm to yourself the following....

Affirmation:
I am full of faith, so much so that it's flowing over to other people.

Repeat the affirmation.
Do this until your predominant feelings are faith and certainty—instead of doubt. This exercise is simple, but when done often it detaches the synapses in your brain that keep you in the pattern.

Doubts can only be removed by action.

—Johann Wolfgang Von Goethe

All is well.

59

It's Enough—I Am Enough

If you ever wonder if you are doing enough to manifest your dreams, ask yourself some key questions.

- Am I procrastinating? If yes, get moving. If no, go to the next question.

- Is this the right path? If yes, keep going. If no, identify your doubts by first connecting to your heart. Take a deep breath, close your eyes, and ask your higher self. Depending on the answer you receive, start moving or re-plan and make an adjustment.

- Could I be doing something to achieve my goals faster? If yes, determine what those things are—keep it simple and do them. If no, let go of the judgment and keep moving.

- Am I missing things that would help me get to my goal more easily? If yes, explore what those things might be. If no, stop overanalyzing and take action.

Those are just a few examples of what can come up as you move toward your dreams. If this was helpful take a few minutes now to come up with your own questions. Then answer them using the same format: "If yes, ..." and "If no, ..." My hunch is that you'll learn a bit about yourself and how to keep moving despite your old, patterned thoughts.

It is enough. It's always enough. Even when it doesn't feel like enough you'll learn something from that, too.

Affirmation:
I am enough. It is enough.

Enough can only be enough to those who believe it's enough.

—Auliq Ice

This Can Take You Out

Perfection is the willingness to be imperfect.

——Lao Tzu

There are many experiences in life just waiting to tease your ego and mess with your life. There are egoic patterns and habits that you can let run wild and they will eventually take you out—throw you off balance.

Perfectionism is a harmful behavior when it is fueled by the need to please others. It is unproductive when it is driven by regimented expectations, rules, and demands. In its healthy form, perfectionism means being conscious about your choices, thinking them through, making the best decision, and doing your best. This kind of perfection is aligned with Source.

All of the topics in this section are big, bad behaviors that can truly make or break your happiness and success—perfectionism, frustration, resistance, overwhelm, procrastination. If they are done repeatedly, they can make you sick. They are very strong emotions that can give you gray hair and high blood pressure!

The great thing is that you can change them.

Worry not.

60

Overwhelm

Sometimes you have so much going on that you convince yourself you just can't do it all. Honestly, that is bunk. Just break it down, one step at a time. Step back, take a few deep, cleansing breaths, and focus on the next step. You can do it.

Overwhelm is the ego's way of making sure you stay in drama. Drama implies that you are extremely important. It implies you are critical to the work at hand and that you are key to making it all happen. No. Just say no to the ego. Remove overwhelm with your breath and take one affirmative action that moves you forward.

Let go of what doesn't need to happen right now. Just let it go. Prioritize one thing at a time. You are more important than the drama. You are the key to becoming calm. You are the master of how you spend your energy. You are in control—not your to-do piles, not your perfectionism, not your ego. You are.

Affirmation:
I am in control of my moment-to-moment choices.
I choose peace.

Nothing splendid has ever been achieved except by those who dared believe that something inside of them was superior to circumstance.

—Bruce Barton

61

Perfectionism

Let's get this clear. Perfectionism is not the same thing as perfection.

Perfectionism is a human, personal requirement driven from the ego that demands perfection and won't accept anything less.

Perfection is a quality of being. In spiritual terms, you are already perfect as a divine expression of God.

Here, we're talking about the things that can take you out. Perfectionism is a state of being that burns energy, creates strong demands on you and others and has the power to make you completely ineffective.

Perfectionists can rarely be pleased, as they hold such a high standard that it can seem impossible to do good work. Perfectionists are extremely hard on themselves and because of that they are never satisfied—it's never enough (which in the eyes of the universe is lack).

Surrender your perfectionism and accept things as they are. That doesn't mean giving up or doing shoddy work. It means letting go of the small stuff and ceasing to be so intensely particular. Excellence is the act of excelling. If you turn perfectionism into excelling to do your best work and let it be enough, you're training yourself to trust in the perfection of the universe.

You are human. Humans make mistakes so they can learn. Get into the flow of creativity, surrender, joy, laughter, grace, and ease by letting go of the things that don't really matter. You are perfect as you are, in all your ways of being and doing.

Affirmation:
I am perfect as I am. Things are perfect as they are.

Perfectionism is not a quest for the best. It is a pursuit of the worst in ourselves, the part that tells us that nothing we do will ever be good enough—that we should try again.

—Julia Cameron

62

Procrastination

Procrastination is a way for the mind (ego) to distract you from following through. It is a form of resistance that takes energy from you. When you repeatedly procrastinate over long periods of time you actually drain your energy.

Why do people procrastinate? Anxiety, low self-esteem, and lack of self-confidence contribute to procrastination. We procrastinate because we feel bored or perhaps don't value a task. Our procrastination becomes a problem when we don't apply discipline and commitment. Instead, we give in to impulses like finding something better to do.

Think about a pile of paper that holds many to-dos. You move the pile around, occasionally look through it, reorganize it, but you don't deal with the actual tasks. How do you feel the next time you look at the pile? Does it drain your energy? Does it make you feel a sense of guilt or frustration?

The trick with procrastination is to start with one small thing, one small step. Pick one thing out of the stack and deal with it. Then see how you feel. Keep doing this, at least once a day, until your pile is gone. When you create a simple practice you trick the mind. You bypass the ego and actually get things done. Try it and see if it works for you.

More energy (vitality) is your reward for keeping your commitments. Doing what you say you're going to do keeps you in alignment with your own integrity and can give you a sense of accomplishment.

Affirmation:
I act now. I follow through on my intention in this moment.

Nothing is so fatiguing as the eternal hanging on of an uncompleted task.

—William James

63

Conflict

Conflict is never fun but it can be a great opportunity to practice your ability to maintain peace and love in your heart. In the face of conflict, the ego wants to jump in, lash back, judge, blame, and make the other person wrong. It wants to be right.

If the ego takes control of a conflict and a battle ensues, there will either be a lose-lose or a win-lose. Neither of those options is best for the people involved. A conscious person has the ability to resolve conflicts for a win-win.

Conflicts are a mirror. They reflect what is going on inside of you. When you resolve your own issues, issues with others will resolve in turn. If you allow too many conflicts to pile up in your life, your life-force energy will begin to drain.

To move forward and out of conflict, be decisive. Choose your battles carefully, as all battles may not be worth your time and energy. Agree to disagree, which means that everyone exercises free will and chooses their own way. We don't have to see eye to eye with each other, rather, enjoy permission to have our own unique perspectives. Choose peace.

State your truth as you choose empowered words that matter. Speak in the highest vibration possible. A friend just shared a great statement recently: "Speak from your heart and be done with it." This is great advice and a phrase worth remembering when faced with conflict.

When faced with conflict, conscious people

- are not easily triggered; and if they are, they go straight to work on the self
- respond instead of reacting
- don't match energy, they stay calm and still
- take responsibility quickly
- apologize first
- listen intently for understanding before jumping in
- are silent when necessary
- look for a balanced win-win solution
- can turn the other cheek
- hold their heart open for resolution

When presented with a conflict, ask yourself, "Do I want peace or do I want to fight?" Do you want less stress or more stress? Less learning or more learning?

When you are conscious in the midst of conflict, you can then lead others to resolution by modeling a higher choice.

Affirmation:
I choose peace. I choose peace. I choose peace.
I choose love and a win-win scenario.

He who does not strike nor makes others strike,
who robs no nor makes others rob, sharing love
with all that live, finds enmity with none.

—Buddha

Think before you act.

64

Frustration and Anger

Let's be honest. There are times in our lives when we just can't stop the frustration from rising, even with our best intentions. Frustration can dive to anger—one of the lower frequency choices of consciousness. Anger is not an act of personal power. It is a demonstration of being out of control. It is a false sense of power driven from the negative ego. When you own your personal power, there is never a need for anger.

> I have learned through bitter experience the one supreme lesson—to conserve my anger; and as heat conserved is transmuted into energy, anger controlled can be transmuted into a power which can move the world.
>
> —Mahatma Ghandi

What causes frustration and anger for you? By what do you find yourself frequently triggered into frustration?

We've learned all kinds of tips to bring ourselves back to center. This tip will be a bit different. Frustration brings up an edgy energy that makes our cells shake, rattles our nervous system, and makes us feel out of control. So how do you get easy with frustration, turn your anger into more peace, and bring yourself back to center?

Always, the first step is to breathe—take three slow, deep breaths drawn from the depth of your root, your base chakra. Breathe in as if the air has the power to cleanse you of stress, drama, and edginess. Just breathe. Keep breathing until you can feel yourself calming to a state of peace.

Now, focus on where the frustration lives in the body. Is it the heart? The throat? The head? Find where it lives. Talk to it. Ask it questions. Find out what the emotion of frustration is trying to tell you. Listen.

Your body's wisdom will lead you to what's really going on. Once you hear the story the body is trying to tell, you can release the energy by breathing in, focusing on this place in the body, and allowing it to release into the moment of now. Now is perfect, still, and peaceful. Keep breathing and receive the feeling of peace.

All is well. Repeat as often as necessary.

Affirmation:
I am at peace and I am releasing all that I no longer need.

Anger is like a chariot careening wildly. He who curbs his anger is a true charioteer. Others merely hold the reins.

—Buddha

65

Resistance

Resistance is a funny thing. When you experience resistance it feels as though you're moving through tar in slow motion, as if you're running headstrong into a thick wall of bubble gum. You run at the wall full force knowing there will be pushback and that you won't know where you'll end up, but you do it all the same.

Kenneth J.M. MacLean, in his book *The Vibrational Universe*, says, "Resistance is a pushing-against; an offering of thought in opposition to something you have observed or experienced. Because thought interfaces directly with the human energy field, resistant thought will cause a descent on the Emotional Scale." For our purposes here, we can refer to the Map of Consciousness (see practice 11, *Raising Your Vibration*).

First, to move through resistance you must recognize that you're in resistance. This feels like agony, frustration, pain, stuckness. If you're in resistance long enough it will cause physical pain. The trick is to know when you're in resistance. Once you know, shine light on it. Sit with the feeling in the body, breathe into it, and allow for some relief.

Second, ask yourself quality questions to help you explore the resistance. Ask questions like,

- What am I so afraid of?

- What is it that I don't want to see most?

- What do I fear is the worst-case scenario here?

When you ask these types of questions you will receive answers.

Third, listen to the answers and embrace them. Ask for more information as you listen. Listen, listen, listen.

Once you receive answers you can begin to release the resistance and move forward. Resistance is the ego mind's way of holding you back from an experience in self-discovery and growth. Remember, the ego mind's job is to keep you safe. Make friends with the ego mind and let it know you will be better off by moving through this resistance.

Affirmation:
I am allowing and living in non-resistance with grace and ease.

You gain strength, courage and confidence by every experience in which you really stop to look fear in the face. You are able to say to yourself, 'I have lived through this horror. I can take the next thing that comes along.' You must do the thing you think you cannot do.

—Eleanor Roosevelt

66

Obligation

When we feel we are under obligation to things in our lives, we open ourselves to the experience of drained energy. Obligation is a negative emotion that links to a belief that we *should* do something that we don't want to do.

So, how do you take obligation and turn it into an empowering experience?

Look at the situation to which you feel obligated and ask yourself,

- What is driving my need to think I should do this?

- What do I get out of delivering on this obligation? What is my motive?

- What would happen if I didn't deliver on this obligation?

Once you've answered these questions, take your obligation and turn it around. See if you can turn it into a desire. Complete the following statement with the payoff or your motive: "I want to do this because...."

Explore what it would be like if you deleted the obligation. How would that feel? Maybe someone is expecting you to do something that you don't want to do. Can you tell them that you don't want to do it? If not, why?

Think about obligation as a choice and see if you can shift some obligations in your reality. You get to choose. You are empowered.

Affirmation:
I choose to serve through desire. I am free of obligation.

Your only obligation in any lifetime is to be true to yourself.

—Richard Bach

How to Use Your Superpowers

I want God to play in my bloodstream the way
sunlight amuses itself on the water.

—Elizabeth Gilbert

There is more occurring inside of each of your human biological cells than you can possibly know. If you choose to practice the ideas in this book, you will find that you are on your way to a life of bliss at a cellular level. Possible? Yes.

What exactly is bliss? It's experiencing God—the Supreme Source running through your veins, overwhelming your heart with love, and rendering you speechless.

This is your Superpower! While it is within you at all times, it's up to your free will and commitment to an enlightened practice that will open doors and integrate this power into your life.

It's all within you. Have faith.

Soar now.

67

You Can Fly

Yes, you can. It's not a myth. You can actually fly! When your soul feels joyous, when it is carefree and not worried about a thing, it soars. The giddiness you feel when you're doing something you love or when you've accomplished something big is a feeling made in flight.

What the caterpillar calls the end,
the rest of the world calls a butterfly.

——Lao Tzu

There are times when you feel as though you're stuck on the ground—due to a heavy fog, ice on the wings, or an extra-strong wind. These are the times to warm up the engine, taxi to the runway, and lift off. It's when the weather looks the roughest that you need to fly the most. Why? Because doing so affirms your resilience. It shows that you can break through your fear. It shows that what you thought was so daunting or impossible was just your imagination running amok.

Now that you're soaring, where is it that you want to go? Flight gives you freedom. Once airborne you're in the world of possibilities. You are in control. You're at the helm of your own destiny. Fly, fly, fly.

A friend of mine who is passionate about flying recently said to me, "When I'm flying I don't give a rip about what anyone else thinks." When she is flying she is free, truly free. Soar, sister! Soar!

Affirmation:
I am free to be me. I am free to fly.

Don't tell me the sky's the limit when I know there are footprints on the moon.

—Paul Brandt

68

Fire in Your Belly

Some days you wake up raring to go. Ideas flourish, your energy is good, and you're ready to create an amazing day. This is fire in your belly—an energy that feels like passion in full force. You're riding the wave of universal flow when you're in this state.

In opening fully to your life and your passions, you will create amazing progress. To use this energy most effectively, keep a notebook or journal to capture your ideas, brainstorms, and tasks you want to accomplish. You can then refer back to these notes if you lose your way or if you need some of your own inspiration.

Some days you would like more fire in your belly but can't seem to access it. Sit with your notebook or journal and write three things that you are truly inspired by or excited about. Then create an affirmation that supports this passion, something like, "I am passionate about changing the life of just one person by listening and providing comfort," or "I am excited to complete this project because it means that it will change people's lives."

It's your time to shine. Now you try.

Affirmation:
I am a blazing source of creation.

The only people for me are the mad ones, the ones who are mad to live, mad to talk, mad to be saved, desirous of everything at the same time, the ones who never yawn or say a commonplace thing, but burn, burn, burn, like fabulous yellow roman candles exploding like spiders across the stars and in the middle you see the blue centerlight pop and everybody goes, "Awww!"

—Jack Kerouac

69

Wind in Your Sails

It's a new day with a new opportunity to be your brilliant self. What would you like to accomplish today that feels natural, easy, and juicy?

If you didn't start your day with an inner meditation, stop and do your breathing exercises (see the 8-Breath ReBoot in practice 30, Breathe to ReBalance). Ah, yes! Remember those? Even three slow, deep breaths can clear your head, initiate flow, and give you energy.

If you are the type who takes big leaps, fantastic! Leap away. Just make sure you go with the flow, pace yourself, and don't overdo. It's easy to get overzealous with our dreams, but it's important to remember that there is a rhythm to unfolding our desires. Trust your heart, ask for inner guidance, and be in partnership with yourself and the natural state of flow.

You might want to re-read the practices on moving forward— with wind in your sails and sun on your face. Pick the ones that inspire you the most, ones that resonate best.

Open yourself to what's next with grace and ease and simply do it. One step, one call, one small effort, and voila! You've made progress.

Affirmation:
I am in flow with grace and ease.

May the wind under your wings bear you where
the sun sails and the moon walks.

—J.R.R. Tolkien

70

Get into the Flow

One of my favorite authors is Mihaly Csikszentmihalyi (pronounced Me-hi-chick-sent-me-hi). Among other topics, Csikszentmihalyi has studied FLOW. Here's Wikipedia's convenient summary of the concept:

According to Csikszentmihalyi, flow is completely focused motivation. It is a single-minded immersion and represents perhaps the ultimate experience in harnessing the emotions in the service of performing and learning. In flow, the emotions are not just contained and channeled, but positive, energized, and aligned with the task at hand. The hallmark of flow is a feeling of spontaneous joy, even rapture, while performing a task although flow is also described as a deep focus on nothing but the activity—not even oneself or one's emotions.[6]

Have you experienced a type of flow where your sense of time disappears? What were you doing when that was happening? When we are immersed in our visions, dreams, and deep, inner passions, time doesn't exist.

Flow is a natural state of mind that occurs when you focus so intensely that it feels like you're in another world. Artists experience this when they are in the full energy of creation. Athletes experience this when they are performing their best feat. Business people experience this when they are living and executing their heart-felt mission.

Find the state of flow. Stay there for as long as possible, and let your manifestations come forth.

---

[6] *Wikipedia*, "Flow (psychology)," accessed April 6, 2017, https://en.wikipedia.org/wiki/Flow_(psychology).

Affirmation:
I am in the stream of flow.

Anyone who has experienced flow knows that the deep enjoyment it provides requires an equal degree of disciplined concentration.

—Mihaly Csikszentmihalyi

71

Willing to Give

In order to give, you must first be able to receive.

—Kenneth J.M. MacLean

True giving is energized by a state of joy, gratitude, and love. It is free from expectations and attachments. True giving is a gift of expansive and generative energy. This kind of giving hurls gratitude into the universe. It has no ties.

As a powerful giver you are full of life force and filled with your own sense of balance, happiness, and joy. In this state your gift has meaning and value. It's done in the energy and intent of giving freely.

Have you ever received a gift from someone who holds conditions, either conscious or subconscious? If you are aware, you can feel in your gut that this gift is not really a gift, it's a bargaining chip. The giver in this case is not giving but loaning, as the gift implies a hidden exchange.

On the other hand, have you been given something from someone who freely gives? The energy of the exchange is so different! It's filled with love.

The universe creates a tension between giving and receiving. It's the yin and yang, the ever-living flow of energy dynamics. If you are a giver and can't receive you quickly go out of balance. You must be able to receive to keep a balance to the flow.

Make it a habit to give and the universe will respond in kind. If you remove expectations of receiving anything in return, you open the potential for an abundant and magical life.

Affirmation:
I give freely of myself in time, energy, and gratitude.

The person who desires to leave things better than he found them, who does more than his share, who is not attached to rewards, who is always seeking to benefit others, who knows he is cared for and rewarded by the Universe for his every effort, is able to act selflessly, without expectation of a reward or a return, without thought of advantage, and of him it is said, "He is better than the best," and, of course, he is greatly rewarded.

—Wu Wei

72

Open to Receive

Receiving is a state of conscious openness. It is a way of being that says *Yes* to the universe—free of limitations and conditions. Your eyes and heart are wide open without defined expectation of the outcomes. If you're not paying attention, you could miss great things coming your way.

In order to be a true receiver you must practice the art of staying open to everything the universe is mirroring back to you—the signs, coincidences, your communication with others, the messages coming through your computer, TV, and radio. The universe uses every energetic medium to speak to you.

As a receiver, you have the ability to discern a perfect vibrational match. In other words, you will identify what feels aligned with your given desire. Remember, the particles moving around you are constructed by your beliefs and perceptions of the world. As an artful receiver you will have positive expectations without being attached to outcomes. As a graceful receiver you will have no definitive expectations, only faith and a knowing that whatever comes is perfect.

Premeditated gratitude is a powerful tool that opens the doors to receiving. Gratitude begets more gratitude. Receptivity inspires more gratitude.

Here's to your ability to receive more consciously and more abundantly, to create more of what you truly want while receiving all that the universe is giving to you.

Once you get used to people giving to you as
much as you give to them and receive all of the
benefits of a less stressful life, you will not
consider putting yourself last.

—Amanda Owen

Be a Co-Creator

To have anything we want, we need only raise our level of consciousness to the level of consciousness where what we want exists.

—Wu Wei

You hold more power than you can imagine. The entire force of the Universe lives within you. It can be a lifelong journey to figure out the rules of this game. If you've read many pages in this book, you're holding the keys to living this life to its fullest, as an expression of God. You are a conscious being with the power to move mountains and truly change the world. It's all within you. Don't buy off on what you see. Co-create what you desire.

You must be the change you wish to see in the world.

—Mahatma Ghandi

You are all that.

73

Make Reality

In the world of co-creation it's commonly understood that we create our own reality, but do we really understand how much of our reality is of our making?

If you believe that your thoughts, emotions, and beliefs create your world, let's explore your reality. Do you like what you see today? Is your reality brimming with signs of your conscious creation, or clues of unconscious happenstance? Are you paying attention?

Make Reality

Take one small step to shift your reality. Imagine or find a picture of something you would like to create today, something small and hold it in your mind. Next, create the feelings you will have as you see this manifestation in your reality. Hold your vision and your emotions steady for roughly ninety seconds. Repeat this throughout your day, multiple times.

Don't allow negative thoughts to intrude into this vision. The key is to truly feel your emotions while experiencing this creation coming into your life. Have faith and know that if this is in your best interest, it will manifest.

Be open and watch what happens ... let go of the outcome. It may not be instant so be patient. Watch as you make it real.

Affirmation:
I am a co-creator with the Universe and I create my reality.

If you have a dream, don't just sit there. Gather courage to believe that you can succeed and leave no stone unturned to make it a reality.

—Roopleen

74

Keep the Faith

Faith means having complete trust and confidence in someone or something. Specifically, faith is a strong conviction in something unseen, and when held with steady confidence it precipitates profound results.

No matter what your spiritual beliefs, there are universal laws at work. When you are in alignment with these laws they reign true in your life.

- When you hold a vision powerfully, without wavering, and back it with the joyful emotions, you affirm to the Universe that this is already so. And the Universe responds.

- If you lose faith, your vision is less likely to occur as you expect.

- Unquestionable faith means to hold strong without question, as if it is so.

- Every thought, feeling, and emotion is heard by the Universe. Be mindful of yourself and your manifestations.

- Everything you desire is available to you. There is no such thing as scarcity. In order to have this experience, it is you who must believe.

- Gratitude and release of outcomes will strengthen your faith. Accepting what is given with a grateful heart will ensure that more is on the way.

Affirmation:
I am holding my vision clearly and with unshakable faith.

Faith is taking the first step, even when you don't see the whole staircase.

—Martin Luther King, Jr.

75

Expect Miracles

A miracle is defined as "an effect or extraordinary event in the physical world that surpasses all known human or natural powers and is ascribed to a supernatural cause[;] such an effect or event manifesting or considered as a work of God[;] a wonder; marvel." [7]

When you expect miracles you open your mind to wider possibilities and to inexplicable happenings that may seem random. Why not make miracles the norm? What if you were to expect them and held yourself open to receive? How many miracles do you think you would see in a day?

Have Eyes of Wonder

Open yourself to miracles. Face your day with wonder. Wonder what will happen and who you'll meet. By doing so you open to the possibilities that are waiting for you.

---

[7] *Dictionary.com*, "miracle, def. 1, 2, 3," accessed April 4, 2017, http://www.dictionary.com/browse/miracle?s=t.

Affirmation:
I am open to miracles. I receive what is waiting for me.

I have found in life that if you want a miracle you first need to do whatever it is you can do—if that's to plant, then plant; if it is to read, then read; if it is to change, then change; if it is to study, then study; if it is to work, then work; whatever you have to do. And then you will be well on your way of doing the labor that works miracles.

—Jim Rohn

76

Leap Often

There is an art to making leaps in life. This begins with discerning your level of tolerance for risk, perceived danger, and the unknown. If you think of taking a leap and your heart races, stop. Breathe into it; ask yourself, "Is this fear real or imagined?"

If the risk is real and would put you in harm's way, your answer may be to stop and refrain from the leap. In most cases though, the risk is not real. Perhaps you're not in harm's way but just feel fearful. Lean into the fear and it will begin to dissolve. Stepping into the fear will diminish its power. Walking through it will prove to you that it was indeed imagined.

If you would like to leap, here are a few tips to practice:

- Determine if the fear is real or imagined.

- Acknowledge the fear and breathe into it until its grip loosens.

- Take action into the fearful step while breathing. (Just do it!)

- Continue to breathe.

- Allow yourself to step forward.

- Talk to yourself and tell yourself, "That wasn't so bad."

- Repeat.

Taking leaps in your life builds muscle for living a fulfilling, abundant, and true life. If you're afraid to take a leap, ask yourself, "How would I feel if I didn't do this?" Leap gracefully into your life.

I have a mantra: "Do one thing every day that scares you." Do this daily and within one month your tolerance for leaping will greatly increase.

Affirmation:
I take leaps of faith in my life.

Faith is almost the bottom line of creativity; it requires a leap of faith any time we undertake a creative endeavor, whether this is going to the easel, or the page, or onto the stage—or for that matter, in a homelier way, picking out the right fabric for the kitchen curtains, which is also a creative act.

—Julia Cameron

77

Fiercely Decide

One of the most powerful actions to move your life forward is to simply *decide*. When you *choose* with strong will and clear intent, you set the energy in motion for what you desire.

The stronger the decision, fueled by conviction, the more likely your desired manifestations are to appear. When you act upon a decision, the forces of the Universe align and the physical world begins to take form in calibration with your intent.

Here are some tips on how to make decisions more easily:

1. BODY WISDOM - When you think about your options, check in with your feelings (defer to your gut). If you think about doing something and your gut feels queasy, that would be a clue toward a NO. If you think about doing something and you feel light, joyful, or at ease, that would be a YES. Use your body as a barometer for your decisions and trust yourself. Your higher self knows the answers.

2. HEART SPEAK - Focus on your heart and settle in until you feel a softening, a quiet, and more peace. As you sit quietly ask the question about your decision, something like, "Is [insert what you're trying to decide on] in my highest and best interest?" Listen for the answer. This will sometimes come softly, sometimes with great volume and intensity. Trust your inner sense to speak to you. When you listen carefully and trust the answer, you have put faith in higher intelligence, your higher self.

3. MIND LOGIC - Sometimes decisions are so big that you need your logic to come into play to feel sure. If this is the case, use a t-chart to assess the pros and cons. List the pros on the left column and the cons on the right column. Let the force of your knowing reveal where you stand and then process your decision through both body and heart.

You will make the decision that's right for you if you trust yourself and your higher knowing—guaranteed. Remember that sometimes the choice will lead us into an experience that is designed for inner growth. Remember to be open to the experience and accept what is given. There is always a higher plan in play.

Affirmation:
I trust my inner knowing to show me the best choice for my highest good.

Remember, a real decision is measured by the fact that you've taken new action. If there's no action, you haven't truly decided.

—Anthony Robbins

Gratitude Is the Key

Gratitude turns what we have into enough, and more. It turns denial into acceptance, chaos into order, confusion into clarity ... it makes sense of our past, brings peace for today, and creates a vision for tomorrow.

—Melody Beattie

One of the most powerful qualities you hold in this life is gratitude. There are a million things to be grateful for and a grateful heart is a giving heart. Showing gratitude is attractive. People want to be with someone who demonstrates the vibrant energy of gratitude. It can make the problems of the world disappear. It can make the worst situation fade away. Gratitude is the elixir of the heart that can turn the grumpiest of men into a gentle puddle of love.

Gratitude is the key to the ultimate lock.

Wear gratitude like a cloak, and it will feed every corner of your life.

—Rumi

Connect with Source, always.

78

10 Gratitudes

We often hear the word gratitude, but when do we *practice* gratitude? When we practice gratitude we make a conscious choice to be in the heart and actively acknowledge those things in our lives for which we are grateful. With a focus on gratitude, tender emotions expand in your heart and attract more of what you want into your life.

Practice Being in Gratitude

1. Start your day deciding to *be* in your heart and see everything with love. This single act has the power to reflect love back to you. It's a circle.

2. Name at least 10 things you are grateful for and focus on the feelings this gratitude brings to you.

3. Keep your commitment—stay in your heart and see only love, the best in everything all day long.

4. At the end of the day ask yourself, "What did the emotion of gratitude show me today and how did it change the outcome of my day?"

5. Then ask yourself, "Am I willing to practice gratitude again tomorrow?"

Love, love, love. It's that simple.

Affirmation:
I am grateful. I am grateful. I am grateful.

The struggle ends when the gratitude begins.

—Neale Donald Walsch

79

Be Love to Gain Peace

From your first breath today to the last breath before you sleep, live with gratitude for *everything* that is present in your life, including the challenges. This level of gratitude creates an open heart and an energy that attracts more of what you want.

Develop a practice of gratitude for the gifts that accompany your irritations or challenges. This will not only ease the suffering but will minimize any negative emotional and physical manifestations that may follow. The secret is in the love.

It can be demanding to love things that irritate you or make your life more difficult, but there's a great secret here: when you do it, your distress melts away.

Turn Irritation into Love

For this practice, identify three to five things that are irritating you, challenging you, or making life difficult. Choose to love them all day.

Loving it all will bring you peace.

Affirmation:
I am loving *all* of my life, *all* circumstances that I have created.

Feeling grateful or appreciative of someone or something in your life actually attracts more of the things that you appreciate and value into your life.

—Christiane Northrup

80

Kindness

As you become more skilled at stepping back, taking a breath, and centering, you open a door to deep kindness for the self. Kindness is the act of stopping all judgmental thoughts and letting things just be. Loving, nurturing, and doting on the self is salve for the soul. Kindness is centered in your heart and is accessible to you at all times.

Kindness Cures

If you need more kindness in your experience today, practice sitting in the heart. Breathe, in and out, while softening your heart by thinking of something you dearly love.

As you do this, notice what thoughts, images, and feelings come up. Let any negative thoughts float by and welcome all positive thoughts. Focus more on the positive. What loving thoughts can you bring up in your heart?

Sitting with these loving thoughts instigates kindness toward the self and then toward others. Kindness is a powerful energy, an expression of love.

Be kind to yourself and watch the world be kind to you.

Affirmation:
I am loving and kind to myself at all times.

You can search throughout the entire universe for someone who is more deserving of your love and affection than you are yourself, and that person is not to be found anywhere. You yourself, as much as anybody in the entire universe, deserve your love and affection.

—Buddha

Your Mindful Practices

Sow a thought, and you reap an act;
Sow an act, and you reap a habit;
Sow a habit, and you reap a character;
Sow a character, and you reap a destiny.

—Samuel Smiles

It's one thing to read a book. It's another thing to actually apply the lessons. In this section, my challenge to you is to take your reading beyond knowledge and into wisdom and action.

You're about to create your bliss plan—a plan that is designed with your unique path and most urgent growth in mind. The moment you decide to become an intentional co-creator, you set the universe in motion to fulfill your wildest dreams. The trick is, you must follow the rules in this book in order to make those dreams come true.

Decide, commit, be consistent, get still, listen, receive, give, and love. Hold the highest vibration of which you are capable. Rise above conflict by responding rather than reacting. Keep your heart open, be grateful, and receive all that the universe is desiring to give you.

Bliss is found in the expansiveness of your heart and the continuous presence of love. It is limitless and has no words. It is within you, waiting for you.

Bliss is who you truly are, your divine purpose. It already is.

Bliss now.

Create Your Bliss Plan

You never change things by fighting the existing reality. To change something, build a new model that makes the existing model obsolete.

——R. Buckminster Fuller

Bliss Consciousness Is within Reach

Beyond *positivity* is a euphoric experience that is indescribable. Sean Meshorer, author of *The Bliss Experiment*, has this to say about bliss:

> What is bliss? It's a hard question. That isn't because bliss is vague, inchoate, or unreal, but rather because it surpasses the capacity of language. Bliss is so vast, boundless, and immeasurable that it encompasses every possible word or definition ever invented—and then some. This is, of course, why we continue to stress that bliss must be personally experienced, not just discussed. Like so many aspects of life, bliss is not readily apparent to our senses. Because bliss is not an object or a thing, our faculties of sight, hearing, touch, taste, and smell are not designed to detect it.... My spiritual teacher, Paramahansa Yogananda, explained that bliss is, "a transcendental state of superior calm including within itself the consciousness of a great expansion and that

of 'all in One and One in all.' When that sense of ego, of separation, melts away, a feeling of total connectedness, of no sense of a 'me' separate from all of creation descends, that is bliss consciousness."

Can you create bliss in your own reality? Simply, yes. Between you and your personal experience with bliss is your life story, your beliefs, and perceptions. Not everyone has to go through the dark to get to the light, but some do. It's not a requirement to feel the state of bliss. You can feel a state of bliss by choice and by doing many of the practices in this book.

Building Your Bliss Plan

Your Bliss Plan is your current, committed focus for your inner work. It's quite simple to create your plan, and it's important to know that the results come when you diligently *DO* the practice.

Here are a few questions to ask yourself before creating your plan:

- What do I most want to change in my way of being?

- What do I need most to affirm that I am growing?

- What do I want to master?

- What is most important to me in life?

My Core Values

To create a plan that has meaning for you, it's important to know your personal core values. On the next page is a list of values. Take a few moments and select eight to ten that describe your beliefs about what you value deeply in life.

CORE VALUES LIST:

Abundance	Diversity	Kindness	Resourcefulness
Accomplishment	Duty	Knowledge	Respect
Accountability	Effectiveness	Leadership	Responsibility
Achievement	Empathy	Learning	Risk Taking
Adventure	Environmentally	Love	Romance
Affection	Conscious	Loyalty	Safety
Altruism	Ethics	Making a	Security
Appreciation	Excellence	Difference	Self-Care
Assertiveness	Expertise	Mastery	Self-Expression
Authenticity	Fairness	Mindfulness	Self-Mastery
Authority	Faith	Motivation	Self-Reliance
Autonomy	Fame	Nature	Self-Respect
Balance	Family	Open-	Selflessness
Belonging	Fast Paced	mindedness	Serenity
Bravery	Flexibility	Optimism	Service
Candor	Focus	Orderliness	Simplicity
Caring	Freedom	Originality	Solitude
Compassion	Friendships	Partnership	Spirituality
Citizenship	Frugality	Passion	Spontaneity
Clarity	Fun	Peace	Stability
Cleanliness	Giving	Perfection	Status
Collaboration	Gratitude	Perseverance	Strength
Comfort	Growth	Personal Growth	Structure
Community	Happiness	Pleasure	Success
Commitment	Health	Poise	Teamwork
Communication	Honesty	Popularity	Time Freedom
Compassion	Honor	Power	Tranquility
Competency	Humility	Practicality	Trust
Contribution	Humor	Precision	Truth
Courage	Imagination	Preparedness	Unity
Creativity	Impact	Presence	Variety
Credibility	Independence	Prestige	Vision
Curiosity	Influence	Privacy	Vitality
Decisiveness	Innovation	Professionalism	Wealth
Dedication	Integrity	Prosperity	Well-being
Dependability	Intellectual	Recognition	Winning
Determination	Status	Relationships	Wisdom
Dignity	Intelligence	Reliability	Work-Life
Diligence	Intuition	Religion	Balance
Directness	Joy	Reputation	
Discipline	Justice	Resilience	

My Core Values:

1. _____
2. _____
3. _____
4. _____
5. _____
6. _____
7. _____
8. _____
9. _____
10. _____

Once you've identified your personal core values, identify *WHY* they are important to you. This will inform you of your current perspective on life, based on your life story.

WHY are these values important to me?

Now, with your core values in mind, create your bliss plan. Which practices—selected from 1 through 80—am I focusing on for the next 21 days? Try to select one to three that are doable for you.

1. _____

2. _____

3. _____

Write your intention for committing to this work.

Example: *I commit to doing these practices for 21 days and taking notes daily on my progress.*

_____

_____

_____

_____

Find a journal that you love and take notes every day as you journey through creating a new, conscious habit.

Success Habits

We are what we repeatedly do. Excellence, therefore, is not an act but a habit.

—Aristotle

It's likely that you wake to your day without a plan and leap into action without much thought. There's so much to be done, right? What if you created your own personal set of success habits that stuck, habits that really worked for you?

Here are some ideas for creating success habits that will help you achieve your dreams:

- Wake up at the same time every morning and set your day.

- Wake up in the morning and meditate deep in your heart on your greatness.

- Sit and breathe—slow, deep breaths—for ten minutes.

- Ask questions to improve your performance.

- Listen to constructive criticism.

- Learn from mistakes and incorporate them as key training.

- Fill your day with positivity.

- Integrate a success mantra or affirmation into your day.

- Make a commitment to achieve at least one goal every day.

- Do one thing every day that scares you.

- Eliminate procrastination and just do it.

- Do what you say you're going to do; follow through on your intent; keep your commitments.

- Commit your goals to paper, and put the list in a place where you'll see it.

- Surround yourself with positive, successful people.

- Show up early to appointments so you have time to ground, focus, and be your best.

- Maintain a fit and healthy body.

- Take breaks when you need to refresh your creativity.

- Be prepared to make sacrifices.

- Ask yourself good, quality questions all day that are designed to make you better and smarter.

- Listen to your intuition. Take time out to meditate or allow.

- Release what you no longer need before you go to bed.

- Spend time with people you love.

- Now, you add some….

These are just some ideas to help you create your own list of success habits. What activities make you feel successful when you do them?

Keep your list of success habits brief and doable, especially at first. Develop a few habits then add more as you feel ready. That said, always stretch yourself to create more until you feel you are in the groove with your best performance.

Quick Access Practices

Sitting in the Heart

To Sit in the Heart, follow these steps:

- Sit comfortably and quietly, free from distractions.

- Breathe deeply at least three times, in and out—breathe in peace, breathe out stress.

- As you begin to relax, focus on your heart and chest region. You may notice sensations that you would like to change. Maybe a heavier feeling is in your heart or a tense feeling. If you have an emotion you would like to clear, use the Sacred Holding practice (found in practice 30, *Forgive the Self (Sacred Holding)*, and later in this section).

- Think of an experience that brought great joy and love. Focus on all aspects of that experience until you feel your heart start to expand. As it opens, it will feel like it is getting bigger. Let this happen naturally. Keep focusing on your joyful, loving experience for as long as you like.

- This is *sitting in your heart*.

11

Raising Your Vibration

David Hawkins wrote a book in 2002 titled *Power vs. Force: The Hidden Determinants of Human Behavior*. This book appeared at the forefront of our understanding of how emotions create vibrations. What I find most intriguing about this book is Hawkins' Map of Consciousness. The map shows the scale of emotions and their vibrational equivalents. Through the use of kinesiology or muscle testing, one can test vibrational levels.

The scale ranges from 20 to 1,000. The highest 300 points of the scale represent an indescribable or enlightened emotion. The bottom of the scale relates to the emotion of humiliation (shame). As you can see on the following page, there are various emotions in between. Abraham-Hicks and other experts have revealed this type of emotional chart and method of seeing, indicating that we may be vibrating when experiencing an emotional state.

The goal, of course, is to try to raise our vibration—allowing us to live in a greater state of joy (or 540 on the scale, which correlates to a very-high vibration). At a minimum we can strive for 250, which is the emotion of trust (neutrality). Here is a basic representation of the scale:

700 – 1,000	Indescribable (enlightenment)
600	Bliss (Peace)
540	Serenity (Joy)
500	Reverence (Love)
400	Understanding (Reason)
350	Forgiveness (Acceptance)
310	Optimism (Willingness)
250	Trust (Neutrality)
200	Affirmation (Courage)
175	Scorn (Pride)
150	Hate (Anger)
125	Craving (Desire)
100	Anxiety (Fear)
75	Regret (Grief)
50	Despair (Apathy)
30	Blame (Guilt)
20	Humiliation (Shame)

Determine where you are vibrating by using your body as a kinesthetic-feedback tool. Here's how:

1. Stand, feet firmly on the floor. Close your eyes and ask your body to show you a YES. Let your body move in the direction it naturally wants to go. In many cases your body will fall forward for a YES.

2. Next, with your eyes closed, ask your body to show you a NO. Your body may fall backward. Whatever direction your body falls is your own internal compass for your NO.

3. To determine your vibration level, ask this yes-no

question: "Using the Map of Consciousness, is my vibrational level above a 20?" Give your body time to fall in its natural direction. Continue to moving up the scale until you reach a NO. Then you will know which general vibrational level you are at presently.

Note: Your mind can alter the outcomes of this method if you let your ego get in the way. Stay unattached to the outcome and set an intention to know the truth.

Try to raise your vibration at least one level, if not more, at one time. Do this by focusing on a memory that resonates with that particular emotion. For instance, to move from shame to grief, allow yourself to cry, release, and let go. Then test your vibrational level again to see if you've moved up on the vibrational scale.

Move up as many emotional levels as you authentically can. You'll notice that if you get yourself up to 250 you are at neutrality. This is a great goal if you're living in the lower vibrations. Sometimes it just takes one step toward a higher vibration to start the ball rolling.

Notice that when you're in the lower vibrational frequencies you attract others who are also vibrating at those frequencies. When you're feeling poorly it's best to connect with beings who are vibrating at higher levels.

Affirmation:
I am raising my vibration now, one step at a time.

29

Breathe to ReBalance
(8-Breath ReBoot)

Do the following to perform the **8-Breath ReBoot**:

- Access some fresh air.

- Breathe in slowly, through the nose, for a count of eight.

- Hold the breath for eight counts.

- Make an "O" with your lips and bend forward as you slowly exhale through the mouth for eight counts—flushing impurities from your body. Push energy from the pit of your stomach. Lean forward and push out any remaining air.

- Return to an upright position. Hold no breath for eight counts.

- Repeat three times, or more if you feel you have a lot to release.

As you do this breath work, pay attention to the energy moving inside you. Allow any emotions that you no longer need to arise. Then release them.

Affirmation:
I am grounded, calm, and centered.

30

Forgive the Self
(Sacred Holding)

For the practice of **Sacred Holding** do the following:

1. Close your eyes and take three slow, deep breaths, releasing what you no longer need.

2. Bring an instance of pain/suffering/judgment into your consciousness.

3. Feel it in the body. Tune in to where you feel this pain.

4. Now, sit with this pain, witness it. Hold your attention on the emotion. It will begin to release or dissolve.

5. Once the emotion has released from your body, try to bring it up again. If there is still emotion, sit with it again until it releases. Do this until you can no longer bring it up.

Affirmation:
I release myself from self-judgments.
I release the need to criticize myself. I am forgiven.

You can do this!

About the Author

When you have a dream you've got to grab it and never let go.

——Carol Burnett

Tamra Fleming was born to be a transformation catalyst. She is a change agent who thrives on inventive and non-traditional solutions, with a knack for spotting future trends. She uses her intuitive skills to bring forth the candid truth to help her clients see what they can't.

She has over sixteen years of coaching experience—helping individuals, couples, and businesses get clear on their purpose, vision, and roadmap to realizing their goals and dreams. She has coached CEOs and business owners in real estate, financial management, public relations, and residential construction to name a few.

Presently, she is an Executive Performance Coach and works with business owners and leaders who want to excel while embedding their core values into their work and businesses. She follows a conscious business model, where relationships, communication, and demonstration of high integrity behaviors are the basis for leadership and company culture development.

Tamra has a vast array of work experiences from seventeen years in the corporate world, as the creative force behind training and development programs for Macy's, Liz Claiborne, Inc., and, lastly, Starbucks Coffee Company.

She was the Founder and CEO of a start-up transformation business for your life and space, which included an online profiler for your life and space, and an academy to train and certify life/space coaches.

Tamra also completed a one-year solo journey around the world where her spiritual awakening was stirred in the sacred mountains of the Himalayas. She also co-created *A Spiritual Gathering*—a monthly spiritual education and entertainment group exploring spiritual practices for the intentional human.

She holds a BS in Organizational Development and Retail Merchandising, as well as certifications and training in coaching, leadership, feng shui, face reading, and various healing modalities.

Tamra works with individuals and small businesses to co-create transformation from the inside out.

She lives in the Bitterroot Valley, otherwise known as Hamilton, Montana.

www.upswingbook.com

Contact Info:

Tamra Fleming
P.O. Box 840
Hamilton, MT 59840
tamra@upswingbook.com

Contributors to the Story

Our life stories are like intricately woven blankets, each thread of a new experience creates a unique design. The threads of my life story have been graced by my teachers, mentors, healers, ministers, coaches, and guides. Their lessons and love are everlasting.

When the student is ready, the teacher appears.

From My Trip Around the World

Rahul Bharti, ancient healing teacher in Kathmandu, Nepal and Pondicherry, India.

Lhamo Dolkar, Tibetan healer and channel of Dorje Yudronma, Kathmandu, Nepal.

From My Training and Certifications

Cathy Hawk, mentor, coach, and teacher, Denver, Colorado.

Lillian Bridges, feng shui and face reading teacher, Kirkland, Washington.

Jean Haner, feng shui and face reading teacher, Bellevue, Washington.

Eric Dowsett, space clearing teacher, Bellevue, Washington.

From My Spiritual Journey, Healing, and Personal Growth

Jamal Rahman, Sufi spiritual teacher and mentor, Seattle, Washington.

Michael Toms, spiritual sage, New Dimensions Radio (now transitioned).

Marie-Rose Phan-Lê, spiritual teacher and healer, Hawaii.

Hope Van Vleet, Intuitive Spiritual Counselor, San Rafael, California.

Dell Morris, spiritual teacher (now transitioned).

Kendra Thornbury, mentor, Boise, Idaho.

My Dear Soul-Sisters and Spiritual Co-Creators in Life and Work

Pattie Hanmer, healer, artist, Feng Shui Practitioner, Vashon Island, Washington. We co-created personal transformation events, collaborated on home interior makeovers, feng shui, and a myriad of personal healing events.

Nicole Kincaid DeDamm, energy clearer and Feng Shui Practitioner, Seattle, Washington. We co-created Entresoul, a life/space makeover business and traveled together on this great spiritual adventure.

Carrie Morgan, extraordinary coach and business counsel, Boise, Idaho. We co-coached and collaborated on many transformational projects.

Sharon Crawford, coach, healer, project management master, and marketing magician, United Kingdom. We partnered on many projects, co-designed and led telesummit trainings, and continue to brainstorm our next moves in life.

Sandi Hanson, spiritual co-creator: A Spiritual Gathering, Terrebone, Oregon. We co-created A Spiritual Gathering— spiritual education and entertainment group exploring spiritual practices for the intentional human.

Bibliography

Bridges, William. *Transitions: Making Sense of Life's Changes.* Cambridge: DeCapo Press, 2004.

Chopra, Deepak. *The Seven Spiritual Laws of Success.* San Rafael: Amber-Allen Publishing, 1994.

Ekman, Paul. "Paul Ekman's Taxonomy of Compassion." *Greater Good—The Science of Meaningful Life* (June 2010). http://greatergood.berkeley.edu/article/item/paul_ekmans_taxo nomy_of_compassion.

Green, Glenda. *Love Without End, Jesus Speaks.* Sedona: Spiritis Publishing, 2002.

Hawkins, David. *Power vs. Force.* Carlsbad: Hay House, Inc., 2002.

Horner, Christine. *Embracing Mindfulness, Your Life's Purpose, and the Leader You Were Born to Be.* Dayton: In the Garden Publishing, 2015.

Keltner, Dacher. "The Compassionate Instinct," *Greater Good— The Science of Meaningful Life (March 2004).* http://greatergood.berkeley.edu/article/item/the_compassionate _instinct.

Levoy, Gregg. *Vital Signs: The Nature and Nurture of Passion.* New York: Penguin Group, 2014.

Neff, Kristin. *Self-Compassion.* New York: William Morrow, 2011.

MacLean, Kenneth J. M. *The Vibrational Universe: Harnessing the Power of Thought to Consciously Create Your Life.* Ann Arbor: Loving Healing Press, 2006.

Meshorer, Sean. *The Bliss Experiment: 28 Days to Personal Transformation.* New York: Atria Books, 2013.

Millman, Dan. *The Laws of Spirit: A Tale of Transformation.* Tiburon: H.J. Kramer and Novato, 1995.

Prophet, Elizabeth C. *Access the Power of Your Higher Self.* Gardiner: Summit University Press, 1997.

Salzberg, Sharon. *Loving Kindness.* Boston: Shambala Publications, Inc., 1995.

Stevens, Robert T. *Conscious Language: The Logos of Now, The Discovery Code, and Upgrade to Our New Conscious Human Operating System.* Asheville: Mystery Systems Books, 2007.

Stone, Joshua D. *Soul Psychology.* New York: The Random House Publishing Group, 1999.

Stone, Joshua D. and Rev. Gloria Exclesias. *The Universal Laws of God,* vol. 1. Lincoln: iUniverse, Inc., 2002.

Taylor, Dana. "What's a Lightworker to Do?" *Supernatural Living with Dana Taylor* (November 2016). https://supernalliving.com/2016/11/15/whats-a-lightworker-to-do/

Taylor, Madisyn. "Dark Night of the Soul." *DailyOM.com* (March 2017). https://www.dailyom.com/cgi-bin/display/printerfriendly.cgi?articleid=57263

Walmsley, Joanne. "Number 80." *Numerology—the Vibration and Meaning of Numbers* (June 2011). http://numerology-thenumbersandtheirmeanings.blogspot.com/2011/06/number-80.html

Wattles, Wallace. *The Science of Getting Rich*. Public Domain. https://en.wikisource.org/wiki/The_Science_of_Getting_Rich

Wilde, Stuart. *Silent Power*. Carlsbad: Hay House, Inc., 2005.

Wei, Wu. *I Ching Wisdom: More Guidance from the Book of Answers*, vol. 2. Rev. ed. Malibu: Power Press, 2006.

Made in the USA
Middletown, DE
22 August 2019